A Woman First: First Woman

A Woman First:
First Woman

A Memoir

SELINA MEYER

ABRAMS PRESS, NEW YORK

Library of Congress Control Number: 2019931287

ISBN: 978-1-4197-3353-6

eISBN: 978-1-68335-411-6

Printed and bound in the United States

10 9 8 7 6 5 4 3 2 1

ABRAMS The Art of Books
195 Broadway, New York, NY 10007
abramsbooks.com

For Richard Splett,
the only person who never let me down

CONTENTS

AUTHOR'S NOTE

Welcome!

I am so pleased that you have purchased this book. I hope that you have as much fun reading it as I had writing it!

Before we get started, I'd like to issue a few caveats and establish some ground rules.

As we know, all great literature was written quickly. There is simply no way that incredibly long books like *War and Peace*, *Crime and Punishment*, or *Madame Bovary* could have been written over one person's lifetime (not to mention along with a lot of other books) were they not written fast. In writing this book, I have attempted to follow in that great tradition.

While those justifiably well-regarded books are fiction, mine is something completely different: fact. But it is a special kind of fact that bears a bit of explanation. Because there is a trade-off between capturing the particular feel of a moment in time—especially when one is "on a roll"—and being scrupulously, tediously accurate, I have chosen to try to tell you the "larger truth" of what my impression was about what happened, when it happened, why it happened, where it happened, how it happened, and who it happened to. If there are any errors or omissions, I am sure that they are trivial, and I will endeavor to correct them for the paperback and international editions or else in another book.

It would, of course, be deeply inappropriate for a president to write the official history of her (or his!) own presidency, due to the tendency of our human natures to ignore uncomfortable, inconvenient, and unflattering truths. So do not think for a moment that this book purports to be an official, critical biography. However, I have done my best to face the facts about myself, and I offer myself up to the reader with nothing hidden and as I really am, not as I might always wish to be.*

Finally, in attempting to offer you "Selina unadorned," I have included a certain amount of frank talk. I think you will find that though there is some very occasional coarse language, it is never used gratuitously and has been employed sparingly in the interest of reporting a sentiment accurately and when there were no other viable options. Nevertheless, since this book is intended for a family audience,† I have removed key vowels from the words in question so that adult readers may experience my account with w-rts and all, while children will be left with a more sanitized, age-appropriate impression along with, perhaps, some awkward questions for their parents and teachers.

So, enjoy! I envy you the journey you are about to take through my life. I only wish I could do it all again myself and maybe change just one or two little things. See if you can guess what they are.

---

* I think the work of future historians should also be taken with a grain of salt, since third parties aren't necessarily any more reliable than the subjects of books themselves. A lot of people have a lot of agendas and are out to get other people. Never forget that.

† Children are our future.

PROLOGUE

From the moment I entered the the White House, I felt like I was, quite literally, stepping into history. Not simply the history of the presidents who had gone before me, like Washington, Lincoln, etc., but the history that I was making myself and bringing with me and which I would leave behind for future generations.

I remember the moment with crystal clarity. It was February 6, 2016, the birthday of singer Celine Dion and former Major League slugger Jose Canseco, as well as Liberation Day in the Philippines. The weather in the nation's capital was cold and clear, with some high scattered clouds forming around sundown, and the daytime high temperature hovered around 17 degrees Fahrenheit (or about −10 degrees Celsius). Fortunately, the winds were mild, at 9 to 12 miles per hour, and from the northeast. The dew point was more or less irrelevant, since the relative humidity was an exceptionally low 6 percent.

As I began to walk the short distance from the office in the Eisenhower Executive Office Building that I had been using as vice president to the Oval Office in the world-famous "West Wing," I reflected upon the much longer journey that had brought me to this historic moment. A journey that had begun some forty-seven years ago in rural suburban Maryland, where a little girl with the unusual and occasionally unfortunate name of Selina (it had proved just a little too close to "Smellina" for some second graders) was born and raised.

For those of you who have never had the pleasure of visiting Eastern Maryland, Centreville is as all-American as apple pie on the Fourth of July. Our neighborhood was a true melting pot of religions (everything from Methodist to Episcopalian), races (it seemed like half the diplomatic corps lived within half a mile), and political beliefs, be they Democrat or Republican. We had bankers, we had doctors, we had businessmen, we had small businessmen, we had people who took care of horses—pretty much every profession under the sun was represented.

Service was a way of life in our town—service to country and service to community. Every year, dozens of candidates would step up to run for seats on the zoning board, even though there were almost never any vacancies. Let me tell you something: If you want to see true democracy in action, just turn up on the second Tuesday of the month for a Centreville zoning board meeting. There's so much shouting, you'll think you've walked in on one of those plays where people curse at each other about real estate being put on by a theater for the deaf. But while I might wish people watched their language a bit, especially when seniors are present, I can't fault their passion.

At home and then at boarding school, I was taught that one simple rule, the so-called Golden Rule, would serve as a nearly infallible guide for how to be a good person and live a good life. "Do unto others as you would have them do unto you," it says.

In order to apply this rule in daily life, one must learn another rule: "Decide what you want from others so that you may give it back to them in accordance with the Golden Rule." And from the very first, I knew what I wanted from others: I wanted to be respected. I wanted to be admired. I wanted to be included. And in order to accomplish these things, I was willing to be hated and feared. "Let them hate you, as long as they fear you," is a third famous rule. A bit less golden, perhaps, but much more realistic.

The journey from little Centreville, a town so small that it was not served by any sort of mass transit (which, let's face it, can bring in an undesirable "element") to where I now found myself, partway between my old office and my new one, had not been easy. In fact, every hardship I had faced and overcome along the way was compounded by the simple fact that I was a woman. It's often been pointed out that when a man is ambitious and assertive he's considered strong, whereas when a woman displays those traits she's called "pushy" or a "b-tch" or a "shr-w" or a "h-rpy" or a "n-g" or a "c-nt" or a "w-tch" or a "wh-re" or a "bl-est-cking" and so on.

As I approached the elevators, I could not help but notice that, despite the efforts of some of the kind of pushy women that nobody, including me, likes, most of the portraits on the walls around me were of men. It was almost as if those dignitaries from days gone by—cabinet secretaries, ambassadors, senators, and, yes, even presidents—were staring at me with their beady eyes and bushy muttonchops and saying, "Go back! Go back, Selina Meyer! Go back to where you belong in the vice president's office! A woman can't be president! Go back!"

(By the way, a lot of people think FDR was very open-minded and liberal, but his portrait was right there with the others, saying the exact same things.)

It was all I could do not to turn back and retrace my steps across the quarter of the hallway from my office to the elevators that I had already walked. But then I thought of the brave women—white, black, and especially Native American—who had sacrificed so much in order for me to get this far down the hallway to the Oval Office. And, more importantly, I thought about how much I had sacrificed and how hard I had worked, how I had gotten here entirely on my own, how I had gotten here in spite of the many people in my life, including my family and staff, who through outright opposition, subtle undermining, or sheer incompetence had attempted to thwart me.

So when I reached the elevator, I squared my shoulders, took a deep breath, and said, just audibly, "You're on your own, Selina Meyer. Right where you've been all along. But you got this far. And that ain't bad."

Ahead of me lay a short elevator ride, another pretty long hallway, then a short walk across the private street that runs between the Eisenhower Executive Office Building and the White House, then another hallway, and after that . . . the Oval Office itself.

I was ready.

A Brief History of the Meyer and Eaton Families in North America

The story of my family is the story of America. Like her, we have known good times and bad. We have persevered, fortified with nothing more than our hopes and dreams, and seen those hopes and dreams fulfilled—but also sometimes dashed. We have known financial setbacks, we have fought wars, we have been forced to displace others from land that we ourselves wanted for the grazing of livestock. From humble beginnings, we have grown to greatness. And like America itself, we have always believed that our best times are yet to come.

The patriarch of my father's family, Deacon Josiah Archibald Eaton, arrived in America aboard the ship that followed the *Mayflower*. My longtime associate Mike McLintock likes to say that the ship was called the *April Shower* because, of course, "April showers bring May flowers," although, now that he thinks about it, that joke would make more sense if Josiah's ship had come first.

The ship Josiah actually boarded in Portsmouth, England, on what was probably a rainy and very likely windy morning in the spring of 1623 was actually called the *Good Fortune*. It has proven to be my "good fortune" in writing this book that there is a long-established society of descendants of the passengers of the *Good Fortune* in this country who have published several exhaustive histories of the voyage and its passengers in order, perhaps, to make it clear that they were every bit as distinguished and accomplished as the passengers aboard the slightly earlier *Mayflower*, who have received the bulk of the publicity and about whom every schoolchild is still taught to this very day at the expense of other people who were just as good.

To the Good Fortune Society, I am indebted for much of the history that follows, which I am using with their express permission (but with some of the words changed) as long as, in their words, I "actively promote the story of the courage and fortitude of the men, women, indentured servants, and slaves of the *Good Fortune* and redress the historic wrong of their having been so unjustly overlooked."*

Little is known for certain about Josiah Eaton before he boarded the *Good Fortune*. His origins have been variously described as "the town of Bakewell in the South of England," "the hamlet of Musktide in Wales," or "the small village of Gravesend in Cornwall." His parentage is equally obscure; his father, Cornelius, is described in different source material as a blacksmith's apprentice, a saddler's boy, and something called a "bagwright," which seems to be a now-obscure profession involving the sewing of different sorts of bags.†

Although he is listed on the passenger manifest as a deacon, there is no extant record of Josiah Eaton having taken holy orders of any kind or receiving any religious training or having been ordained in

---

* *The History of the Good Fortune and Its Passengers*, Harriet Gilchrist and Jordan Mcleod, fourth edition, Boston, MA: American Genealogy Publishing, 1966, page 1.

† In the interest of full disclosure, I should mention that some genealogists have suggested that the "Josiah Eaton" who sailed on the *Good Fortune* was actually an entirely different man with an entirely different name who assumed the identity of Josiah after being accused of witchcraft.

any established church. In fact, the only contemporaneous mention of him in legal documents is a mere two imprisonments for debt, an extended bankruptcy trial, eleven prosecutions for fraud, and forty-one corporal punishments (ranging from whipping to confinement in the stocks) for poaching. In the face of this scant evidence, it is difficult to say what kind of man he was. It is possible that given the various forms of nonconformist religious fervor sweeping the Western World at the beginning of the seventeenth century, he merely conferred the title of deacon upon himself, feeling entirely justified by the new ways of religious thinking in doing so. That he was a man of deep faith cannot be doubted, for why else would he set out upon such a dangerous journey to what was, in those days, very much a New World?

Josiah's fellow passengers on the *Good Fortune* were, like their predecessors on the *Mayflower,* mainly ascetic pilgrims belonging to one of the many sects of that first flowering of early Protestantism, and their motivation for the arduous journey was a simple search for religious freedom. There were undoubtedly some adventurers and even some scoundrels among them, since the Merchant Adventurers investment group, who funded the voyage, would have foreseen the necessity for some practical and even ruthless men if the colony was to be sustained and to prosper.

Josiah appears in Captain Heneage Mountjoy's invaluable logs several times in ways that clearly indicate that he was, by the standards of the day, very much a free thinker. On July 7, 1623, for example, the captain notes that "the rogue Eaton has again caused mischiefe by malignantly setting fire to a rival churchman Horatio Underwood and berning [*sic*] off of his leg." Later that same month, on July 22, the log entry "the bosun confronted that devil Eaton after finding him again in the quarters of the unmarried ladyes having exposed his nether regions and instructed several of the women to place a kiss upon his man part" suggests that Josiah had already begun the search for a wife while still in transit.

Finally, a violent dispute over whether the bread and wine were actually transubstantiated into the body and blood of Christ at the Eucharist resulted in the death of one of Josiah's fellow churchmen, the Reverend Phineas Forrest, and the disappearance of his slave, Cato, who was presumably lost overboard in the fray, as well as the forcible rape of three young women. As a consequence of this, Josiah reached what would become the Massachusetts Bay Colony on October 28, 1623, with his legs in chains and his reputation in tatters.

And so it was to be a long climb up for Deacon Eaton!

After the drama of that epic voyage, Josiah, his children, and grandchildren settled down to build new lives in early Colonial North America. In this they were aided by the cardinal virtues of Pilgrim industriousness and thrift as well as the comity and fellow-feeling that characterized these hearty bands of stalwart pioneers living in isolated settlements. Thanks also to a spirit of forgiveness as well as the bottomless need for able-bodied men, Josiah did not remain in chains long.

It is difficult to overestimate the hardships of this time. The six generations of my family born prior to the Revolutionary War bore a total of 2,418 offspring, with each of the women giving birth to an average of ten children before dying and being replaced by a second, younger wife, who would give birth to an average of ten children, and so on and so forth. Of these 2,418 infants, 616 died before their first year and an additional 702 did not live to see ten years. After the age of ten, the mortality rates became more favorable without ever becoming actually favorable. At least 491 died in the epidemics of unexplained fevers that periodically swept the Colonies along with the constant chronic plagues of dysentery, cholera, bacterial infections of all types, and actual plague. Poor nutrition and a lack of trained physicians, not to mention general pre-Enlightenment ignorance, turned even the most minor affliction into a virtual death sentence. A hard-nosed doctrinal view that death and disease were sent by God to punish sinners made caring for ill family members almost sacrilegious among certain overly zealous branches of the Eaton family.

Add to all that the general air of violence and mayhem that beset the New England frontier. A great number of premature deaths resulted from conflict with Native American tribes who, though they have surely suffered greatly since, have much to answer for regarding their conduct during and immediately after their first contact with white Europeans. More than three hundred Eatons were scalped, tomahawked, bound and drowned, flayed, or burned alive before the Mohawks and Wampanoags were ultimately pacified. Many others simply disappeared in the historical record, and surely many of those fell prey to Indian mischief.

When the Native Americans did not slaughter my ancestors outright, they often kidnapped them and held them for ransom or sought to raise them as members of their tribes. One famous example is of Rebecca Eaton, my great-great-great-great-great-great-great-great-great grandmother, who was taken by a band of Mashpee Indians while playing draughts outside her family's farmhouse in Duxminster, Massachusetts, in the summer of 1667. Through an intermediary, their chief, Malauwaupeg, offered to return the girl for a ransom of flints, sewing needles, "spice" (by which, presumably, he meant salt), and ax heads. Rebecca's father, Richard Eaton, declared that he would never pay any ransom and that the Indians were welcome to the girl, whom he described as an "ill-tempered mumchance fractious childe."

The Indians who had taken Rebecca soon found themselves very much in agreement with her father and, in the end, were able to persuade him to take her back only by giving him a dozen beaver pelts, worth an enormous sum at the time.

And so, when all was said and done, barely twenty-five of my early ancestors lived to be forty and fewer than ten made it past fifty. Perhaps that is why ambition and precocious achievement have always run strong in the Eaton blood. For as the Early Eatons were living and, more often, dying, they were also building, exploring, and serving their communities. To put it another way, they had developed a taste for politics.

The men of that era distinguished themselves by service in colonial militias, those stout predecessors of the Minutemen, who gathered at a moment's notice when the alarm was sounded to shoot their matchlocks and flintlocks ineffectually at stealthy Indians or noisy animals or others of their own number who had attempted to outflank an imaginary enemy and wound up being mistaken for their nonexistent foe. Those who by dint of owning property were allowed to vote voted, and they sometimes ran in local elections or sought appointment from the king's representatives. In this pursuit they were often frustrated by the petty jealousies of others who would dispute their qualifications and sow dissension behind their backs. Still, some were elected, and one, Arthur Eaton, even held comparatively high office as private secretary to William Trumbull, the debauched governor of the Massachusetts Bay Colony, but this seems mostly due to the fact that Governor Trumbull was wont to pleasure himself with Arthur's wife, Caroline, and sometimes also with Arthur's daughters, Martha and Winifred, and sometimes with two of the ladies at the same time, and occasionally with all three. For these purposes, Trumbull was inclined to keep Arthur Eaton and his attractive family close at hand and thus was moved to grant him the prestigious appointment.

As the years passed, the Eatons spread out from the point where they had disembarked from the *Good Fortune*, though some remained within one hundred yards or so for a century or more. Some traveled west to the very edges of Massachusetts, where they found the residents' casual and self-centered style of living not to their liking and soon returned. Others journeyed to the genteel Old South, where the plantation culture and economy were beginning to emerge. Here these prodigal Eatons found much to like, and many settled down, spawning new branches of the family, among them the Eatons of Virginia, the Eatons of the Carolinas, the other, less good Eatons of Virginia, and the Wagners of Virginia, who were obliged to change their name as a consequence of some legal misunderstanding.

Although our Southern cousins never achieved the renown of the Washingtons or the Jeffersons, they still considered themselves to be people of high social standing, a position they sought to maintain through a financially complex process of purchasing, selling, and repurchasing slaves. What had quickly become apparent to the Southern branch was that social standing was measured by the number of slaves owned, and, almost as quickly, they determined that while the total number was important, few took note of the actually quality of the slaves. With their canny Yankee trading skills, they managed to develop a secondary market for old and infirm slaves who could be purchased at a steep discount and yet counted toward a family's total slave headcount and thereby enhanced the family's social position.

In some ways, as has often been true in our family's history, the Southern Eatons were victims of their own success. As their secondary slave market prospered and grew, it became increasingly obvious to their more established neighbors what they were doing, and with the characteristic snobbery of provincial country gentry as well as the aristocratic disdain for anything that smacks of sharp dealing, the Eatons were shunned and forced to move on. Still, in those days of the young nation-yet-to-be, there were always new horizons and social-climbing planters eager to claim high slave counts much the way the modern, status-conscious suburbanite will brag about the square footage of his McMansion and offer to show you his wine cellar.

The tumultuous years of the American Revolution brought change and, with it, as the Chinese proverb teaches us, opportunity. It is here in 1776 at one of history's great inflection points that we shall leave behind the story of the Eatons generally and focus on my branch of the family in particular.

The Eatons have always answered the call to our nation's service, whether it be responding to a census, filing tax returns, serving on juries, voting frequently, or being conscripted into military service Samuel Eaton was the first of our family's many soldiers to achieve distinction on the battlefield. Rising from a humble private to become General Benedict Arnold's aide-de-camp, Colonel Eaton played an essential but somewhat behind-the-scenes role in the eventual unmasking of Arnold as a traitor.

In reviewing contemporary accounts of the Arnold affair, sources are divided as to whether Samuel Eaton's conduct in encouraging General Arnold to betray the British in order to expose him was a masterpiece of wily cunning or merely good fortune, and a court-martial seemed similarly perplexed. Nevertheless, in the end, even George Washington admitted that "the rascal Eaton has done the nation some service in betraying the betrayer before he himself could be betrayed."

Two generations or, as one wag put it, "four score and seven years" later, Samuel's grandson Major Morgan Eaton, a Union Army veterinarian, was mentioned in dispatches from Second Bull Run, where in less than ninety minutes he amputated more than two hundred limbs from men both wounded and healthy. On the other side of the Mason-Dixon Line, another of Samuel's grandsons, Corporal Bradley Eaton Moorhouse, served with distinction as an orderly for Robert E. Lee and is credited with having created Lee's distinctive hairstyle. After the Civil War, Bradley continued to serve Lee for the remainder of his life, setting out his clothes every morning, arranging flowers and interior furnishings in a way that Lee found pleasing, and continuing to barber and dress his hair. Family legend has it that Bradley Moorhouse handled the embalming, dressing, and final cosmetology of Lee's corpse and that a framed handful of gray hair that for years hung on the walls of his descendants' homes had come from Lee's body, moistened, it was said, by the copious flow of Bradley Moorhouse's tears.

In later life, Bradley Moorhouse changed his name to Robert E. Lee Jr. and became a star attraction in the traveling circus of Morris Monk, a competitor to P. T. Barnum, whose sideshow was considered almost as good.

World Wars I and II brought with them new experiences, new friends, and exciting opportunities for foreign travel. An emerging family tradition of service in the Quartermaster Corps found many Eaton cousins ensconced behind the lines, working diligently and often without much thanks to ensure that the troops in their care were supplied with, as Floyd Eaton put it in a letter home, "both soup and soap and I'll be damn-d if I can tell the difference!"

On my mother's side of the family, her father, Howard Norris Melville, was a notable personality of the Gilded Age, beginning as a rent collector for J. P. Morgan, eventually becoming a stockbroker specializing in the nascent chemical industry, and finally being named a partner in the venerable investment bank First Boston. His mother, Dorcas, was a central figure of one of the great scandals of the era when she left his father and briefly became the Countess of Belgravia after marrying a visiting British nobleman, Gerald, the seventh Earl of Belgravia, then on a tour of the United States, who was eventually exposed as one Stanislaus Poniciewicz, a penniless Polish immigrant and bigamist. The meeting of five different "Countesses of Belgravia" in a courthouse lobby forms the basis for Edith Wharton's acclaimed short story "The Countesses' Lament."*

After Poniciewicz's sentencing to ten years in prison, Dorcas Melville took to her bed, declaring that the only person she ever loved was "my poor Stanny." She never wavered in her affection, even after he returned to her upon his release from prison and stole her life savings of $14,000 (the equivalent of $45 million today if invested in Apple stock at the right time) and a framed lock of Robert E. Lee's hair.

It is said that Colonel Melville never forgave his mother for the teasing at school he was forced to suffer as a consequence of her indiscretions but that nevertheless he sought to please her, claiming, as her lover the bogus earl had, to have earned various fictitious distinctions, including degrees from Harvard and Yale, the ownership of a magnificent country house of which he showed her many pictures (it was actually the local high school), to be a descendent of the writer Herman Melville, the author of *Moby-Dick*, and to be a colonel in the U.S. Army as well as a general in the Mexican Army.

It is possible that this genetic gift for prevarication assisted my grandfather in his rise to a position of significance in the capital

---

* Being deceived by bogus European noblemen is a bit of a family tradition for the Eatons, as you will see in a few paragraphs and also later in Chapter Twelve: On the Run Again—Campaigning in the "Real" America.

markets of his time. A bit of doggerel from the *Knickerbocker* sketches describes him thus: "Let's hear a cheer for Colonel Melville / Of honey'd words yet fork'd tongue / Ne'er met a stock he couldn't sell / And 'twill swindle the Devil when he gets to Hell."

My mother, his only child, was raised in an atmosphere of comfort and privilege in Darien, Connecticut. Her mother, the colonel's wife, Caroline Calvert, a fragile, vaporous woman of delicate constitution,* was called "Dips" or "Dipsy"—short for "Dipsomaniac"—and spent most of her days indulging a boundless enthusiasm for motion-picture magazines, reading them over and over and cutting out pictures of movie stars to make elaborate collages in which the stars appeared to be attending a glamorous party at which she was the hostess.† As soon as my mother was old enough she was sent away to school, first to Foxcroft, where she developed a powerful attachment to Roberto, the handsome bay stallion she was assigned as a member of the school's justly famed equestrian program. After Mother stayed out after curfew and was eventually found asleep in Roberto's stable stall after an extensive search, the colonel ordered Roberto destroyed, for which my mother never forgave him.

In due course Mother went on to Smith and then embarked upon a year of travel and study in Europe with her college roommate, Martha Ostergaard. There she met her first husband, "Prince" Guido Rimaldi, while skiing in St. Moritz. After a whirlwind courtship lasting barely

---

* Caroline Calvert was herself the descendent of a long-established American family whose most famous member was her nephew James, who under the stage name of "Lily de Valley" was a drag queen and a leading light in the glittering world of Paris in the '20s.

† She was also at one point the chair of the fund-raising committee for the Darien Library and a vice president of the Connecticut Junior League, but those were both pretty much no-show jobs and never interfered with her collages.

a week, they were married in a small Alpine church. Two days later, Rimaldi began an affair with mother's friend Martha and then divorced my mother and married Martha. Ten days after that, my mother reconciled with Rimaldi and he divorced Martha. A month later, driving a race car purchased for him as a wedding gift by my mother, he crashed during the Monaco Grand Prix, killing himself and eleven spectators, including four children. The race stewards blamed the accident on my mother, who, it was alleged, energetically waved at Rimaldi while wearing an excessively form-fitting sweater as he attempted to navigate the legendarily hazardous "Widowmaker Squeeze."

After this series of unfortunate events, Mother returned to the bosom of her family in good spirits thanks to certain pharmacological innovations that had recently become popular in Switzerland. Mother claimed for the rest of her life that she deserved credit for introducing Valium, Librium, and quaaludes to the American market and was the first person to discover the compound beneficial effects of mixing all three of these medications with a jigger of bourbon.

Concerned that my mother's heart had not been sufficiently broken by her recent experiences, my grandfather arranged for my mother to begin playing tennis with a young associate of his, Gordon Dunn Eaton, a dashing graduate of the Harvard Business School who had won varsity letters in rowing and tennis as an undergraduate at Hamilton College. Though my father was eager to accommodate my grandfather, who was also his boss, by playing tennis with his daughter, sparks did not fly between the couple. They quickly compromised on a system by which my father would hit a tennis ball against a backboard for forty-five minutes while my mother watched and took tranquilizers. She would later say that once she achieved the proper biochemical equilibrium, she found the rhythm of the ball striking the backboard strangely soothing.

Impatient at being uncharacteristically thwarted in his plan to have my father take his daughter off his hands, Grandfather eventually offered the couple $100,000 (or nearly $80 million in today's money if it had been used to buy a large Park Avenue apartment) to get married. To their credit, both my parents independently demanded that they receive their payments in cash.

As my father's charm, good looks, and evasion of the Vietnam draft brought him steady success in banking, he eventually decided to break ties with my grandfather and set out on his own. Daddy had determined that certain vulnerable public companies could be pushed to the brink of insolvency and then taken over at a steep discount through the rapid purchase of ownership stakes, even if the shares were borrowed. Once the takeover was complete, the company could be rapidly dismantled and the assets and constituent parts sold off in order to repay the loan of the shares and still retain a nice profit.

Ten years after their marriage, my parents relocated to Centreville, Maryland, where, flush from a recent successful corporate raid, my father purchased a 1,400-acre gentleman's farm, Bentcrest. It was in that bucolic setting where, every April 15, after filing one of his famously creative tax returns, my father would initiate his annual sexual encounter with my mother. On one such occasion, perhaps under the influence of a new mix of sedatives, she acceded to his demands, and nine months later, I was born.

A brief word about the family of my ex-husband, Andrew Meyer, whose name I bear. Their origins are shrouded in the mists of Mitteleuropa, from whence they issued forth, fleeing persecution of various kinds. Ashkenazi Jews originally from Galicia in what is now Poland, the Meyers moved first to Transylvania, then Romania, then Moldova, then Greece, then Danzig, then Hungary, then back to Romania, then

Slovakia, then Slovenia, then Lithuania, then Turkey, then Egypt, then Mandate Palestine, then Italy, and then Portugal, before settling in Pennsylvania, where they built a small business selling mildly radioactive patent medicines. Theirs, too, is a quintessentially American story of perseverance and industry, even though it took place mostly in Europe and in some cases in countries that no longer exist.

A Woman First:
First Woman

CHAPTER ONE

Mornings on Horseback, Evenings at the Library—My Early Years

If the boy is the father of the man, then it follows that the girl must be the mother of the woman. Although I am very much a modern woman, I'm not one of these self-pitying, therapy addicts who enjoys spending hours reviewing every moment of her childhood with an expensive psychiatrist in the hopes of gaining new insights into her adult self and perhaps make some kind of peace with her inner demons, fostered in youth but who only began to rear their ugly heads in later life.

I find that sort of thing self-indulgent. And, plus, how much can one really learn about a person from their childhood?

I do not believe that my parents really ever loved each other. They were a product of an earlier time, not so far removed from the days when marriages were arranged at all strata of society as dynastic unions among the great and grand or, for the middle classes, just a way of safeguarding respectability and keeping small family businesses or farms afloat into the next generation. Although she never said so, I have reason to believe that my mother's family regarded my father with some suspicion, thinking his family belonged to a slightly lower caste of the upper class than they did. As the proprietors of a consumer-facing business, the Consolidated Bank of Maryland, Daddy's family was technically "in trade," as my mother's family saw it, and beneath the notice of large landowners like her family, who had built dozens of slums and tenements in Baltimore's depressed Belair-Edison neighborhood to house the enormous influx of Italian and Jewish immigrants who arrived at the turn of the nineteenth century and who carried on in a one-thousand-year-old feudal tradition.

As it happened, both family fortunes were largely wiped out in the Great Depression when my paternal great-grandfather's bank went under (despite his last-minute plea in the fashion of *It's a Wonderful Life* for his friends and neighbors not to withdraw their savings, which led to his lynching), and the Belair-Edison real estate holdings vanished almost overnight when Mother's family hired a team of local arsonists to burn them down for the insurance money in a series of fires that killed eighty-eight. (The arsonists, though extremely reliable in matters concerning arson, proved less reliable partners from a business standpoint and wound up implicating my maternal great-grandfather and his relatives, who narrowly escaped being sent to jail.)

So, by the time the parents met, both families lived in reduced circumstances, and the debate about which one stood higher on the ladder of social distinction had become somewhat academic. That does not mean, however, that the matter was laid to rest; to the contrary, in proof of some deep aspect of human nature, it raged all the more vigorously now that the stakes had all but disappeared.

But, as I say, I never saw my parents fight about lineage or anything else—but neither did I see them hug, and I believe that, even from an early age, I would have been disgusted if I had. By the time I was old enough to think about whether or not they loved or even *liked* each other, they had been leading largely his and hers lives for a decade at least, with Daddy traveling on business or working in the stable he had converted to an office, and mother largely preoccupied with her show dogs and television programs.

What memories I have of my very earliest years are fragmentary and probably mostly drawn from photographs as much as genuine recollection. In the photos, I stare at the camera, unsmiling, at home, on my pony Chicklet, at my birthday party, on vacation at the beach, alone, with my parents, or surrounded by cousins and friends. Although the circumstances changed, my expression never did—proof, I think, of a naturally serious demeanor and a disdain for frivolity that has allowed me to focus intently on the things in life that really matter as opposed to the bottomless distractions of family nonsense.

In the fullness of time, it has occurred to me that perhaps I was an unwanted child, the result, for example, of a drunken encounter where my father, after celebrating the filing of an especially fraudulent tax return, forced himself upon my unwilling mother, who was drunk for some other reason and either powerless to resist or oblivious. But there is a difference between being unwanted and being unloved. If, in fact, I was conceived in the manner I have suspected, then I have the comfort of knowing that my father loved me so much that he made my mother pregnant with me despite her passive, or possibly active, resistance. Daddy forced me into the world in the same way he forced himself on mother, and what greater love is there than that?

It may surprise hopelessly bourgeois and conventional readers that I regard this "origin story" as a source of strength rather than an excuse for self-pity. I knew plenty of kids with families that, at least outwardly, appeared loving and cohesive, and they were, invariably, not the kind of children I wanted to play with or found interesting. My friends, though few in number, were drawn chiefly from the more select group of children of divorce or from families that didn't waste time with too many activities or too much supervision.

We were emancipated from an early age, left blissfully to our own devices, trusted to make adult decisions about when to do homework, when to watch television, when to go to bed, when to come home, when to wake up, whether or not to go to school, and what brand of cigarettes to smoke. Needless to say, we were envied by our neighbors and classmates who had the kind of parents who were always dragging them to playdates, parties, and miscellaneous activities. The furnished basements of my fellow "unloved" "misfits" were in fact the crucible in which my adult personality—strong, independent, curious—was forged.

For most of my childhood, we lived in a large house surrounded by acres of open countryside and leased farmland. On Saturdays during the fall and spring, the local fox hunt, the Berkeley Hounds, would ride through our property and, whenever possible, Daddy and I would ride with them. Although I take what I regard as a "common sense" position on gun control and animal cruelty, I think that, in its own way, there's nothing more all-American than fox hunting. It combines a love of the outdoors, a reverence for tradition, and a determination to eradicate vermin, but does so in a colorful, entertaining, and tasteful fashion. Anyone who has hunted for foxes on horseback knows that there is nothing more exciting than watching a pack of hounds (perhaps assisted by terriers if the fox has gone to ground) corner a wily vixen or dog-fox after a long chase and tear it to pieces. Maybe it doesn't sound beautiful, but I know if you could see it, you'd agree with me. Some of my most joyous memories from childhood are when, after a successful hunt, I was presented with the fox's tail or, in one case, its head. I still have that head somewhere. Must remember to check.

Our property had some of the best coverts in the county, and as both a property owner whose land was hunted and also at one point (until there was some misunderstanding about the allocation of the hunt fees) a Joint Master of Fox Hounds, Daddy had the responsibility for cubbing in the spring, which is the process of digging up the nests and killing some number (usually half) of the young foxes to help ensure that only the most intelligent and energetic animals survive—applying evolutionary pressure on the fox population as a whole. While other girls may have spent their time with their father at a museum or on a bike ride, I was engaged in the far more enriching pursuit of digging up baby foxes and chopping off their heads, usually with the sharp edge of a shovel.

One of my great regrets is that I didn't do more to promote fox hunting and other field sports when I was president. Whether or not you approve of hunting, I think everyone would agree that fox hunting in particular builds character and that character is something that is sadly lacking among the great majority of Americans. I am proud, though, that the two attempts I spearheaded as vice president to secure the Olympics games for U.S. cities (Tucson's bid in 2012 and Cincinnati's in 2014) incorporated fox hunting in its classic form as well as drag, trail, and bloodhound variants as the centerpiece of the American bids.

Whenever I speak to schoolchildren, I stress the importance of reading. Reading is important, I tell them. Always read. When you can. I used to read. Do you feel bored? Then you should read. You'll never be bored if you have something to read—as long as you pick something interesting to read. Who can help you make sure that what you have chosen to read is interesting and not boring? A librarian can help. What about a teacher? Yes. A parent? Sure, also a great idea. The point I try and make with the kids—be they younger kids who are just learning to read in kindergarten, older kids in elementary school who are awakening to the joy of reading an interesting, non-boring book, or older children who have decided that all books are boring and need to be persuaded otherwise even if that effort will ultimately prove fruitless—is that there are lots of great books for readers of all ages, and so it's very wrong to think that all reading is boring. Yes, some books are boring. I don't think anyone who has read a lot of books or not read very many books but made poor choices about the few books they have read, would disagree. What are some good tactics to cope with a boring book when one encounters one? Well, there is no foolproof method. You should probably try and stick with it for a while. But one thing you should avoid, I tell kids, is looking down the page to see when the particular section they are reading that may be boring might end, as indicated, for example, by the indentation of an upcoming paragraph. This tactic for relieving the boredom associated with a boring passage will very often end in heartbreak when the reader sees that, in fact, the boring passage they are reading does not end before the page and could, for all that they know, continue indefinitely, belaboring whatever boring point is being made, perhaps all the way to the end of the book, or even, in the sort of nightmare scenario that will inevitably flash across the wandering mind of a bored reader, beyond the end of the book, boring the person reading the book forever until the end of their life or maybe even beyond the end of their life, across eternity until the heat death of the universe and— who knows?—even beyond that into the realm of alternate universes and their infinite receding event horizons. Religion offers an alternate cosmology in which the clearest understanding of astrophysics about the extent of time and space is subsumed into some even vaster concept of the infinite of infinities—to wit, the mind of God. And yet it is within the powers of a boring book to bore even the mind of God, as God well knows.

Children need to learn early that writers are habitually deceptive in luring unwary readers into their many insidious traps. The most common of these is to entice the reader to buy the book through clever art direction of the cover, or though laudatory encomiums by literary luminaries or other celebrities on the back cover, and possibly, when things go exceptionally well, by appearances by the author on television programs or on *Fresh Air* with Terry Gross. Don't be fooled! Just because a writer has the minimal talent necessary to make their book sound semi-interesting during a conversation with the overly obliging La Gross, that doesn't mean their book is *actually* interesting. The promotion of books by people like Terry Gross is, quite simply, a trail of tears, leaving in its wake as many frustrated and angry book purchasers as it does satisfied ones—perhaps many, many more.

But, of course, the most soul-destroying of the cynical writer's tricks for convincing the guileless reader that the boring part of a book they are reading may be coming to an end is by dividing some exceptionally boring upcoming part of the book into paragraphs that will suggest that the author has changed his or subject and, it is to be hoped, moved on to something more interesting. And yet when the unwary reader actually begins reading the new section, it turns out that the writer has not moved on at all, but has simply deceived the reader through the paragraph-indentation trick or other punctuation gimmicks, and is, in fact, just rehashing the same old dull and obvious point about, perhaps, something that every sensible person would agree with and really doesn't require any sort of elaborate song-and-dance argumentation but which the author is attempting to utilize to garner some kind of unearned praise for appearing to be intellectually or artistically courageous when, in fact, they are just a garden-variety lazy weakling and bore who has attempted to foist a broader impression of themselves as an artistic pioneer in order to be invited to parties where sycophantic throngs will gather 'round to lap up the meaningless drippings from mouths intoxicated by twenty-dollar-a-bottle pinot noir, an overrated wine that most people seem to like for its lack of flavor rather than for its active possession of one.

The point is that I have always loved reading and often used to steal away to read books borrowed from my parents' extensive library. Lots of funny stories having to do with that.

Did I have a conventional girlhood? Most definitely not. Would I have traded it for anyone else's childhood? Not for all the world.

CHAPTER TWO

Confessions of a Popular Nerd Athlete— School Days . . . and Nights!

It is well-known that I have often been called "The Education President." Am I ashamed of this? No! Quite the opposite, in fact. I am *proud* to have been called "The Education President." Of all the many issues that a president can concern him- or herself with, I think a very good case can be made that education is one of the most important. Don't believe me? Well, let's try a little exercise: What do you think is the most difficult challenge we face in the world today? Maybe, for you, it's jobs. Well, you can't get a good job without an education, now can you? I mean, some good jobs, sure. Working turning a crank in a factory for a few months and then faking an injury that entitles you to both a settlement in a lawsuit and a lifetime of disability payments could be considered a good job, I guess, if you want to get paid to spend your life fishing or watching car racing on television, and you don't need much education to fake an injury, one would think. And I suppose, in that case, your crooked lawyer would fill out all the forms for you so you wouldn't really need to know how to read and write or express yourself particularly well.

But that's an isolated case. An exception that proves the rule, if you will.

Let's pick a different policy arena in which to prove the importance of education. How about climate change? You can't do anything about climate change if you don't have an education. You'd need to be a physicist or maybe a chemist to figure out what to do about that. It's a huge, interdisciplinary problem with many facets, so biologists and biochemists also have an important role to play. Geologists a bit also maybe. Archaeologists not so much. And the algorithms that predict complex interactions in the upper atmosphere require the input (no pun intended!) of computer scientists, mathematicians, and statisticians who, like economists, are considered "poor man's scientists." All of these different highly educated people—not just men but also women, too!—have to work together to solve the problem of climate change. Now, to be fair, while these scientists seem to be pretty good at identifying the *problem*, it's not as if they've been terribly great at coming up with *solutions*, despite all their education.

Okay, so maybe that wasn't the best example either. Doctors! Doctors need education. Think about the life of a doctor. Pretty much your entire working life is spent writing. Doctors write hundreds, if not thousands, of prescriptions every day, so there's simply no way you can be a doctor if you don't know how to write. I think we all wish doctors could spend a little more time learning how to write *clearly* so that a prescription for, say, sleeping pills isn't filled incorrectly by the idiot pharmacist so that you wind up with a strong laxative or something. That happened to someone I know, which resulted in her inventing (but tragically failing to trademark) the expression "sh-t the bed."

Here's something they don't teach you in school but is really worth knowing: Take anything a doctor tells you with a giant grain of salt, because I have learned that more often than not they're just lazy clueless losers like everyone else.

Pharmacists are supposed to be educated, but a lot of the time it doesn't seem like they are or, if they are, it seems they weren't educated very well. Don't take this the wrong way, but a lot of them also look like they learned how to do pharmacy in Korea or the Philippines or someplace like that, and God only knows whether they value education as highly in those countries as we do here in America.

Here's something you may not know about pharmacists: The arts and sciences of pharmacy are the second most popular thing for inmates to study in prison after—you guessed it—the arts and sciences of locksmithing. Look, I guess anything's better than giving prisoners even more time to do pull-ups, lift weights, and toss around the medicine ball so that they can become even scarier and more dangerous than they were when they got sent to jail. And as the daughter and ex-wife of men who, due to misunderstandings both on their part but also on the part of law enforcement, very nearly went to jail on a number of occasions, I am a firm believer in second chances and in allowing people to pay their debt to society and get the whole thing over with rather than spend a fortune on legal bills.

All of that said, one kind of education I'm not a huge fan of is teaching prisoners how to pick locks and make drugs. Let me explain my reasoning here. Two of the activities that land people in jail in the first place are burglary and robbery and, if we want to reduce recidivism, I think we should make it harder for criminals to reoffend rather than making it easier by teaching them how to open locks better than they did the last time, when they got caught. The same goes for pharmacy. I mean, on some level, I get it. If we teach prisoners how to make their own drugs or give them better access to drugs by helping them get jobs as pharmacists rather than having to buy them on the street, which can often be a prelude to crime, we might be able to reduce drug crime or, at least, improve the quality of the drug crimes in this country. But I happen to think that it might be best if we tried to keep them away from drugs *altogether* and leave pharmacy work to Koreans and Phillipinesians. Besides, how do we know that inmates who study pharmaceutical dispensation in prison are going to actually try and get jobs in legitimate pharmacies such as Rite Aid, CVS, or, my personal favorite, Walgreens? If those pharmacies were not as deeply committed to second chances as perhaps they should be, then they might not want to hire former drug criminals to be their pharmacists. That would leave these prison-trained pharmacists with nothing to do except manufacture crystal meth in their bathtubs at home—crystal meth that, by virtue of the taxpayer-subsidized prison education, might be far more potent than their competitors'.

The one area of prison education that I do support wholeheartedly is legal education. It makes simple common sense that the best lawyers—the best criminal lawyers at any rate—would have at least some prison experience. The same goes for judges, though probably not Supreme Court Justices because, as with everything, there is a limit.*

My personal passion for education was fostered through my own personal experience with education in the course of being educated

---

* I think people are sometimes surprised to discover that a president, who is charged with governing a whole country and therefore maintaining the, if you will, thirty-thousand-foot view, can also be as detail-oriented as I am, with this elucidation of the key points regarding prison education being a terrific example. Well, that's me. That's Selina Meyer in a nutshell: capable of seeing the big picture while simultaneously getting completely granular down to the microscopic or even electron-microscopic level. This freakish ability, not to mention the conscience-driven compulsion to apply my extremely rare talent to the great issues of our day, has been as much a curse as it has been a blessing—my cross to bear, if you will. But it is a cross that I bear happily, even jauntily, when the sacrifices I make are for the good of all mankind, especially American mankind.

myself. My formal schooling was undertaken at a series of private schools, first Miss Hamly's, then Miss Dotson's, and finally Miss Pakenham's, a small all-girls boarding school with a strong emphasis on character-building through equestrian activities. Miss Pakenham's has been in the news lately, not, thankfully, because of a sex scandal like so many other top-flight boarding schools, but rather because of a "lack of sex" scandal, in which a sexually frustrated senior sued the school for failing to instill in her the sort of social grace and flirting skills that would enable her to meet and engage in sex with suitable or even unsuitable mates. All I can say is that things were *quite* different in my day, back when old Miss Pakenham (the original Miss Pakenham's great-granddaughter) was still alive. She made very sure that her namesake institution maintained exceptionally high standards in all areas of instruction, not just garden-variety "readin', 'ritin', and 'rithm'tic" pedagogy but also etiquette, ballroom dancing, and the other skills that fell under the overall heading of "grace and lady-likeness." While it may seem out of step with contemporary values, Miss Pakenham placed a constant emphasis on how to make oneself attractive to members of the opposite sex in order to find a suitable husband. I sometimes wonder if young women today couldn't use a little more of Miss Pakenham's brand of education.

Of course, learning the innumerable minutiae that make up the corpus of knowledge of what constitutes civilized and ladylike behavior is but a small part of what one needs to know in order to be "popular." One also needs to be on the lookout for more practical insights of the sort that can come from local "townie" girls, who have been admitted as a part of a well-intentioned effort at redressing social disequilibria. At all the schools I have attended, I have found that the awarding of scholarships is very much a two-way street when it comes to who benefits, which explains why I am such a strong supporter of creating greater education opportunities at private schools for poor and working-class students. While the school may offer the scholarship girl or boy an education that is far superior to his or her local public school, the scholarship student, having experienced life through a very different set of circumstances than their classmates, often has a great deal to teach in return. I think that's all I'm going to say about that.

To bring us back to the modern day, once word of the lawsuit (which was settled for a mere pittance, about $85,000) got out, enrollment plummeted and Miss Pakenham's was forced to close. Its demise is a cautionary tale for other schools that may not have committed enough time and resources to teaching their students how to be sexy, as Deerfield and Hotchkiss have always done.

From an early age, I was always a bit of a "nerd," as you can probably tell from what I have written above about my love of reading. But just because I was a nerd, that doesn't mean I was unpopular or antisocial or preoccupied with schoolwork and grades. To the contrary, my naturally gregarious personality, my athletic ability, and my freckle-faced good looks made me among the most popular girls at all my schools. To be clear, these things are a gift from Almighty God, and I am eternally grateful to Him for giving them to me.

I prefer a different definition of the word "nerd," one that incorporates the idea of being popular and attractive and well-groomed in addition to being a good student though not *such* a good student that being a good student defines one in some way. I appreciate that the idea of what a nerd is has changed a bit in recent years, so that it also includes being obsessed with science fiction and superheroes and elves and computer games and things like that, but I was never interested in any of those things and was, in fact, moderately disgusted by people who were. So when I redefine the word "nerd," I am redefining the original, more narrow definition that has to do just with school and hygiene and wearing glasses, which I never did. (And I have always been scrupulous in matters of personal hygiene.)

One of my few regrets from my presidency is that we never got around to putting into effect an initiative I had tentatively entitled "Nerd Nation," which was intended to encourage American grade school and high school students to—in the words of the slogan some of the whiz kids at the Department of Education came up with—"Nerd It Up!" and celebrate the virtues of studiousness. Unfortunately, other than a terrific logo and some PSA announcements featuring successful athletes, actors, and supermodels, the enterprise fell victim to a particularly aggressive round of budget cutting as well as a somewhat mismanaged Congressional hearing featuring testimony from Derwerd the Fur Nerd, a nerd character we had had designed that looked a bit like a young, smaller, and much more green-colored Chewbacca, but with buck teeth and glasses. When it was first suggested by whoever it was who ultimately took the fall for it, I admit I thought Derwerd was an innovative idea and a great way to relate to young people on a level they could understand.

Although the highlight reel of the Derwerd hearings currently has more than one hundred million views on YouTube, and Derwerd became a "meme" in many forms, this was not exactly the outcome we had intended. The mix-up occurred when a young Polish actor was hired to dress up in the Derwerd costume for the hearings by the Senate Committee on Health, Education, Labor, and Pensions. A highly skilled mime who had received many awards at arts festivals throughout Europe and Canada, Tadeusz's English was just rudimentary. He *understood* a great deal but had difficulty responding with any sort of precision. Our intention was that he should respond in mime, which we thought would draw extra attention to what otherwise might have been rather dull and dry hearings. And he did respond in mime. The problem was that, unexpectedly, the questions he was asked were somewhat technical in nature about learning disabilities and regional deviations in educational outcomes and that sort of thing, and Derwerd's attempts to respond in mime quickly devolved into an extended and extremely confusing game of charades. One by one, the senators drifted out until Derwerd was left alone by himself performing an answer to a question about the prevalence of four-year-college going in working class Hispanic communities by pretending to ride some sort of chariot or winged horse.

One of the ironic aspects of the catastrophic Derwerd hearings was that Tadeusz was one of the most attractive men I've ever met in my life. Perfectly built with well-defined muscles but not musclebound, free of tattoos or other blemishes, with long, flowing hair and cheekbones sharp enough to cut glass, he was the very epitome of Slavic beauty. Slavs are unquestionably the most attractive of peoples, and Poles especially so.* Although no brighter than the rest of his countrymen, Tadeusz was just smart enough to understand that his appearance as Derwerd the Fur Nerd before the Senate's HELP Committee had gone less than perfectly and felt terribly remorseful about it.

I met with him a number of times afterward to make sure that he understood that the whole thing wasn't really his fault and that, whenever he needed to be consoled, I felt I had a duty, as the person who had indirectly initiated the whole debacle, to console him. At any

---

* As we all also know, they're not the smartest knives in the drawer, but when they are as gorgeous as Tadeusz was, their national lack of intelligence is easy to overlook.

hour. Though the evenings were generally more convenient because people wouldn't constantly be disturbing us with appointments and meetings and that sort of thing.

More so than any other president before or after, I believe I took the responsibility of the president to be a role model extremely seriously. And as America's first female president, I applied myself to the task of being a role model for America's young women and girls especially seriously. As long as I have been in the public eye, I have hammered home one message, derived from my own life story: To all of those kids out there who feel that they are "different" and don't "fit in" because they are more mature and sophisticated than their peers or more stylish or because they don't "run with the pack" when it adopts some new crazy clothing or hairstyle, I have always proclaimed loudly, "You are not alone!" If being dedicated to my studies without, you know, overdoing it, if balancing schoolwork with ample leisure activities, if maintaining a healthy lifestyle in body as well as mind—even if it is by doing things like yoga rather than more needlessly competitive and time-consuming team sports—if all those things make me a "nerd" well then, I'm proud to say, "I am a nerd!"

CHAPTER THREE

The Greatest Night of My Life—
The 1984 Baltimore Junior League
Debutante Cotillion

When I was growing up, there was a saying I sometimes used to hear at my mother's bridge games or when my father would go fly-fishing with friends while drinking. "Decent people," this saying went, "should appear in the press just three times: when they are born, when they are married, and when they die." This principle, known as "Hatch, Match, and Dispatch" is now sadly very much out of date in our era in which the only thing that is important to anyone is being famous.

That a sort of dignified reticence was once considered a desirable trait is hard to imagine when today's young people court one another by sending pictures of their vaginas back and forth on their telephones, and a certain kind of notoriety, sometimes having to do with these very same vagina pictures, masquerades as fame. I suppose that there have always been vagina-picture-senders among us, but until cell phones became ubiquitous, they were, one hopes, few and far between. In lieu of vagina pictures, generations of well-brought-up young women made a formal debut when they were presented—usually at a white-tie dance—to whatever constituted "society" in their city or region. The underlying notion is that these debutantes were now grown women and, in some sense, available to be courted by eligible young men, one or more of whom would be her escort to the ball, the enterprise nominally benefitting some charity or other.*

Although it was perhaps a foregone conclusion, because my mother had come out there, a few months after my eighteenth birthday I received an invitation to make my debut at the Junior League Cotillion (unquestionably the most prestigious of Baltimore's two Caucasian debutante balls) in the fall of 1985. Preparations were begun immediately on two fronts: a dress and a date. For the dress, my mother and I made a trip into Washington, DC, because my mother believed that Washington, with its large diplomatic corps and busy social schedule, was likely to have a larger selection of suitable gowns than provincial Baltimore. And indeed we were able to compromise on one that met my mother's prime criterion, which was that the dress have a deep enough décolletage to show off my breasts in order, as she put it, "to trick some titty-crazed moron into marrying you and taking you off my hands."

Ironically, in light of later events, we found the gown at Nuefeld's Department Store (long defunct) which was owned by the family of one of my most dedicated early backers, Sally Nuefeld, and also by the family of one of the many women Andrew cheated on me with, also Sally Neufeld. The visit to DC was also important for another reason, which was it was the first time I had visited Washington as an almost-adult and, I have to say, I liked what I saw. Something about the grand public buildings and vast open boulevards awakened

---

* Honestly, I can't believe I have to explain all this, but my publisher tells me that the kind of readers I can expect to buy this book or, God forbid, take it out of the library, will most definitely *not* be the sort of people who really know what a deb ball is—so disappointing.

a spark of latent ambition—a spark that would one day burst into the enormous conflagration that was the Selina Meyer presidency.

How many girls my age, I wondered, visiting Washington in order to buy their debutante gown, looked at all the big white houses and, especially, the biggest and whitest one of all, the White House, and thought, "I could live there one day—as first lady or maybe even first lady *president*!"

And thus the seed was planted.

In the matter of a suitable escort, I was not given any choice, or even consulted. My mother let me know that my date for the evening would be Carlton Westerbrook, the son of a neighbor of ours and business associate of my father's, whom I had known since we were children. Now, Carlton Westerbrook was handsome and athletic and his parents were, even by the standards of Centreville, loaded. He was also a psychopath and always had been. As a baby, he had been strangling stuffed animals and ripping their throats out with his teeth before he could walk.

Lots of kids have interests and hobbies—things like gymnastics, Lego, or learning how to "play" the drums. In almost every instance, these enthusiasms are temporary and fleeting. Carlton was different. He had one main interest, which was raping animals and, eventually, people, and he never wavered in his zeal for it. Field trips to local aquariums, Boy Scout jamborees, Sunday school . . . all could end only one way if Carlton was there: with a sexual assault on a smaller and weaker girl or boy followed by a brief flare-up of scandal that was quickly hushed up by virtue of large cash handouts, a phalanx of scary lawyers, and nondisclosure agreements.

While there has always been a mild sexual undertone to debutante cotillions (cotillii?) in the sense that girls who had come out were now regarded as "available," bringing an incurable rapist as one's date seemed to be taking things a bit far. When I pointed this out to my mother, she conceded that while Carlton had a reputation as "a bit handsy," his parents were lovely people and, by longstanding tradition, a debutante's date could expect, at least, to "get stinkfinger."

After all the local schools, private and public, had declared him incorrigible—as well as numerous run-ins with the police—Carlton was sent to Hillside Academy, a military school with a long tradition of educating Maryland's juvenile delinquents. It was clear to anyone who knew him even slightly that Carlton was headed in one of only two possible directions in life: either to prison or, if his parents' expensive lawyers prevailed, to some sort of mental institution. Before that, though, he would be my date to the Junior Assembly.

Now I will admit that Carlton looked quite distinguished in his ersatz military uniform when he arrived at my house to escort me to the ball. I should explain for the uninitiated that a coming-out party is very different from a prom and miles apart from a garden-variety date of any kind. For starters, one's parents are in attendance for the entire evening and act as the hosts of a table that includes the debutante and her escort, of course, but also close friends and relations. In my case, these were my mother's divorced sister Aunt Lisa, accompanied for the occasion by her gay decorator friend Señor Luciano del Porto (who had been born Ralph Weiner in Fond du Lac, Wisconsin, and whose Italian accent proved fugitive during the course of the evening); our family lawyer, my beloved "Uncle" George and his wife, Maggie; Carlton's father, Ordway Westerbrook (Carlton's mother was an invalid of some unspecified type and rarely ventured beyond her bedroom); and Daddy's business associate Count Pawlenski (who was a local car dealer) and the monoglot Countess, his wife.

We made, in short, an especially glittering group amid the bejeweled ladies and distinguished gentlemen and bright young things who assembled at 7:30 that December evening in the ballroom of the Grand Hotel (now WeWork). But the most beautiful person in the whole room, bar none, was Daddy.

Tailcoats had been out of fashion for more than half a century in 1985 and, frankly, good riddance, right? I mean most men look completely ridiculous in white tie unless they're head waiters or orchestra conductors and sometimes even then. For the most part, the tuxedo has been a marvelous innovation bringing as much joy to humanity as the light bulb or laptop computer for the simple reason that almost all men look pretty good in one. And, don't get me wrong, Daddy looked great in black tie also but he was one of those rare beings—one in a billion, maybe—who looked especially ravishing in tails.

Daddy had always been a good-looking, well-groomed, immaculately dressed and shod male of the species. Some may have gone so far as to call him a dandy or peacock, but I think the care he took about his appearance was really an expression of the goodwill he felt for his fellow men. Daddy truly dressed as though he were his brother's keeper. And what brother would not be proud to be kept by such an elegant keeper!

From the time at which the planning began in earnest and the actual night of the event, I had always regarded my debut with a measure of ambivalence, even indifference. It was a foregone conclusion that I, like my mother before me, would come out. I had known that ever since I was old enough to read and enjoy the *Social Register*. But as the big night approached, I have to say I was dreading the whole thing a bit, especially, I suppose, the seeming inevitability of being sexually assaulted by Carlton Westerbrook. The only thing I was really looking forward to was spending an evening with Daddy, in white tie, where I would be the center of his attention.

Carlton, like all the boys, got drunk early and got drunk hard. His duties—the formal ones, anyway—were minimal. He was expected to march with me in a sort of structured dance-like thing when the debs and their beaux all paraded around and bowed to the assembled throng. And he managed that with only a few stumbles. He was also expected to dance with me and the other ladies at our table, but after a brief first dance when I rebuffed his attempts to pull my dress up so that he could slide his hand into my underpants, he devoted all his attention to my Aunt Lisa, who seemed more open to that sort of thing.

Daddy, I noticed, seemed to be refilling Carlton's drink frequently and, at one point, I thought I saw him ask Aunt Maggie for a small capsule which he broke open and dissolved into Carlton's glass. Carlton's father, who had described the entire event as "faggot nonsense," had left early and offered my mother, whose work, she felt, had ended as soon as the evening began, a lift home, which she readily accepted. The other guests drifted away, including, eventually, Aunt Lisa and Carlton, who snuck out to have sex in the bushes, with Aunt Lisa returning alone about twenty minutes later covered in Carlton's vomit. From long experience, Señor del Porto was a master of this sort of situation, and he quickly spirited her away, as well, leaving me alone with Daddy.

The rest of the night was a glorious, heavenly blur. It seemed to me that the air had never smelled sweeter, Lester Lanin's music had never been gayer, and the Grand Hotel ballroom had never looked more like a prince's palace where I, for one night at least, was Cinderella. We must have danced twenty dances together, first the waltz and fox-trot, but then, as the party got looser, a mambo and a tango, and we even joined an exuberant conga line. The last five songs were all rock 'n' roll standards, and Daddy and I twisted the night away until the lights came up and, as the rising sun slowly brightened the east, it was time to go.

It was the greatest night of my life, and nothing before or since has matched it nor could anything mar it—even the next morning when Carlton was found lying in the bushes outside the hotel face down in a puddle of frozen vomit with his pants around his ankles, dead of exposure.

CHAPTER FOUR

Of Age I Come

From the time I was born, it was a virtual certainty—a foregone conclusion, if you will—that I would attend Smith College, as my mother had and her mother had before her. A private, all-female liberal arts college founded in 1871, Smith was nestled comfortably in the bucolic hamlet of Northampton, Massachusetts, where it had remained largely unbuffeted by the tribulations of the tumultuous '60s.

I arrived, a dewy-eyed freshman, in the fall of 1985. Daddy had driven me up in his beloved but temperamental Citroën, and we had been forced to stop overnight at the house of a college friend of his, a charming divorcee or maybe a widow or maybe an old friend whose husband was away on business, by the name of Mrs. Loomis, who lived in a large comfortable farmhouse in rural New Jersey. We got a late start the next day and by the time we arrived at Hubbard House on Green Street, I found my roommates already in residence.

To my delight, I saw that one of them was a familiar face or, at least, a face that looked familiar. It was Wendy Booth, whose sister Libby had been a counselor at Tee-Mo-Too-Ket, the equestrian summer camp I had attended for six years. I could see by her carefully chosen, tasteful outfit and her comfortably sporty hairstyle that she and I were birds of a feather and would be friends for life.* It quickly emerged that our mothers had been friends during their time at Smith and had actually dated twins at one point. Wendy and I flipped a coin to see who would have which bunk. I lost and had to take the upper bunk, but Wendy graciously offered to take it instead. That was the kind of person she was.

Slouched on the room's only single bed, which she had already claimed for herself by virtue of having arrived first (she lived pretty much around the corner), was our third roommate, Barbara Maldonado, and she, unfortunately, was a very different sort of person. I'm not saying Barbara was a *bad* person, exactly, just that her background had not perhaps prepared her to fully appreciate the myriad little courtesies that, put together, constitute a gracious mode of living and, indeed, behaving.

Although Barbara had clearly chosen her outfit with care, the individual garments themselves were just, well, cheap. Her flowered T-shirt seemed better suited to an evening alone on the sofa while the rest of her laundry was in the wash and the jeans she was wearing were of a brand hitherto unknown to me. Without visible embarrassment, she explained that she was first person in her family to attend college. Her father owned the local Shell station in Northampton and her mom worked as a secretary in a doctor's office.

Hmm-hmmm. So.

Both Wendy and I had perked up at the mention of a mother who worked in a doctor's office, hoping that, if he were a dermatologist, we might be able to get facials or, when necessary, cystic acne treatments for free or, at least, at a steep discount. As a second choice, we were hoping for an obstetrician-gynecologist who, of course, could be

---

* She later became a disciple of the Bhagwan Shree Rajneesh and we lost touch.

helpful in the event of yeast infections, crab lice, or, God forbid, an unwanted pregnancy.

So you can imagine our disappointment when we learned that her mother was a secretary for a pediatrician, the most useless kind of doctor of all. And while Wendy and I had both been promised Volkswagen Rabbit convertibles at the start of our sophomore years (another coincidence!), neither of us had cars as yet and thus were unable to take any sort of advantage of Mr. Maldonado's presumed auto-mechanical skills.

But the bigger problem with Barbara was that, as someone from a public school background, she lacked the polish that comes when one's rough edges are burnished through exposure to what is unfashionably referred to as "society." Barbara had never been to a formal dance other than a very tragic-looking high school prom that she insisted on showing us pictures of while Wendy and I struggled to stifle our laughter. She had not attended camp, being too busy working as a lifeguard at the town beach (although she really did not have the figure for lifeguarding work, in my view), and her social life seemed to consist mostly of, as she called it in her broad New England accent, "passing the puck" around on a frozen lake with her four older brothers. It was this supposed ability to "pass the puck" that had led to Barbara's being admitted to Smith in the first place, since the school was in the midst of one of those big "equality" crazes to which liberal colleges are chronically prone, and it was attempting to start a girls' ice hockey team, as if anyone would want to watch that.

Naturally, Barbara had never made a debut. Wendy had come out the previous winter, as I had. In her case, she had made her debut at the International Debutante Ball in New York, which my mother always regarded as a bit showy and tacky, but I guess, though I loved her, Wendy always had a bit of that side of her, as well. When we tried to explain the significance of being a debutante to Barbara it was like talking to someone who spoke a completely different language or was a deaf-mute. She just didn't get it! I mean, she understood the basic idea of dancing in a hotel ballroom to Lester Lanin while wearing formalwear, but the whole notion of formally establishing one's eligibility to be courted by young gentlemen of a similar social station seemed to her to be bizarre and, as she put it, "old-fashioned." Ah, well, some things just can't be explained to some people, if you know what I mean.

My freshman year proceeded in what I guess was the normal manner for the time. I took basic courses in English, European history, French literature, and art history and joined a modern dance group. (Decades later, my daughter, Catherine, would join a modern dance group at Smith, as well, but hers was just idiotic hopping around.) I went to football games and fraternity parties at Amherst and, occasionally, Williams. Like all freshwomen, I was photographed in the nude by the renowned scientists William Herbert Sheldon and Earnest Albert Thomas as part of the prestigious Ivy League Posture Study. Both professors complimented me on my excellent posture and said that I was a perfect illustration of their theory that the higher one was on the social hierarchy the better one's posture. To this day, my daughter's slouching still offends me. I find it so unnecessary.

I read recently with some sadness that most of the photos of nude Ivy League college freshmen and Seven Sisters freshwomen had been destroyed by the Smithsonian. I know for a fact that I must have looked pretty darned good in my picture, especially compared with a lot of the other girls, and I am very sorry that my pictures no longer exist. In the years since, as I rose higher and higher in office, I have always voted against funding for the Smithsonian for this very reason

College was, for me, a time of learning, to be sure. But it was also a time of love. It was at Smith that I met the first three great loves of my life. Three-and-a half, I guess, if you count my ex-husband, Andrew. If frank talk about human sexuality offends you, well, read no further.

Howard Biddle III was the son of an ambassador and the grandson of a governor. His family businesses, Biddle Petroleum and Biddle Mining along with Biddle Shipping and Biddle's Department Stores, controlled a significant portion of the U.S. economy. Tall, handsome, and immensely popular, a junior political science major and a varsity letterman in both lacrosse and water polo, I first caught sight of him across the room at a "Pimps and Hos" party at the Chi Psi house at Amherst. Resplendent in a mauve pimp outfit, complete with wide-brimmed hat and two-tone shoes, Howard was the cynosure of all eyes, including my own. What a perfect pair we would make, I thought. Him, rising steadily through the world of business or diplomacy, maybe even becoming president. And me, right there at his side—like Jackie O but with a better sense of personal style.

Of course, I was not the only Smith girl with a sneaker for Howard Biddle, although I was probably the only freshman with the courage to have a crush on him. And there were other girls at other colleges, miserable whorehouses like Mount Holyoke and Wellesley, who were always circling, their beady eyes on the man that was rightfully mine.

I resolved that I would win the heart of Howard Biddle, no matter how steep the odds, and, in order to do so, I would devise a clever multi-stage plan. This was my first attempt at a campaign of any sort, and the experience that I was to gain through it would serve me in good stead during the many campaigns to come.

Job One was to determine Howard's schedule so that I could be wherever he was. This was obvious, and I could expect my rivals to have come up with the same plan. The process of spending as much time as possible in his vicinity in the hope of a serendipitous encounter was made more difficult by the simple fact that Amherst and Smith, though nearby, are different colleges, and a woman by herself tended to stand out on the Amherst campus except during home games when there was so much hustle and bustle that it was possible to move around unnoticed. The obvious solution, of course, was to dress as a man and enroll at Amherst under an assumed name, the "Yentl strategy," if you will. But after a weekend of experimenting with wardrobe and hairstyling with the assistance of the estimable Wendy, I had to concede failure. I was simply too much a woman, too feminine and womanly, too shapely, and too graceful to ever pass as a man. Curse the fate that brought Howard Biddle into my ken and then kept us cruelly apart!

After months of attending water polo matches and lacrosse games, not to mention parties at Chi Psi, I was still no closer to my goal. We had made eye contact, sure, mostly me contacting the corner of his eye with all of my eyes. But I could still not swear that Howard, my love and my life, knew me from any other nubile young beauty. What was worse, my diligent efforts to meet Howard were consuming most of my waking hours, and as a result my grades were slipping and I was in danger of flunking out. An ignominious unscheduled return to Maryland would put my love almost impossibly out of reach.

I had chosen political science as my major in order that, in the event that Howard and I were ever to meet, we would have something to talk about. I ventured to imagine that the very fact that I was a poli sci major might give us occasion to meet, since it might make me seem interesting to him and like someone with whom he shared interests. I had coerced Wendy, who, though very sweet, had a weak personality and was easily led (as evinced by her joining of a religious cult in later life), into doing much of my schoolwork for me in exchange for borrowing rights to my entire sweater collection. This freed up some but not all of my time for searching for Howard.

As a quarry, Howard also posed particular challenges. He showed a shocking lack of curiosity about the source of the dozens of small gifts and anonymous letters that I sent to him or left in places where he was likely to find them. And he seemed immune to the extraordinary efforts I went to to dress in a manner that he might find pleasing in the event that we were to meet. It seemed a no-brainer to me that a person with Howard's background would appreciate a woman who dressed well—but also with a hint of sex appeal—and who wore a clean, light scent with citrus overtones such as Fracas or Bois d'Hadrien.

Through careful sleuthing, I had figured out his course schedule in a matter of weeks and had posted a large map of the Amherst campus on my wall with colored pushpins indicating where he would be and when. Howard proved more difficult to track during his recreational or study hours, however, because his habits, other than attending athletic practice, were not regular. During this time, my body was covered with scratches and bruises thanks to the many nights spent scrambling through bushes and up and down fire escapes at various Amherst dorms and frat houses trying to catch a glimpse of my beloved. I regarded these nighttime forays as no more than diligent fieldwork of the sort a scientist might do to study an exotic animal in the hope of not alarming it when he (or she! though female scientists were less common back then) finally attempted to capture it. There were more than a few times when I had to send an investigating policeman or security guard after some invented Peeping Tom whom I had just spotted in the neighborhood heading in this, that, or the other direction.

The spring semester ended and summer vacation began without my having exchanged a single word with Howard Biddle other than during phone calls when I declined to identify myself. The summer passed in a tearful and forlorn blur as I paged listlessly through my mother's fashion magazines and imagined our life together as Mr. and Mrs. Howard Biddle. Here we were water-skiing on the French Riviera, then riding in the Queen's carriage at Royal Ascot; one week a formal dinner party at our Park Avenue apartment with some of Howard's important business friends, the next an impromptu clambake in the dunes at Southampton. Our children, Gabriel, the little towheaded boy, and Samantha, the raven-haired beauty who was the very spitting image of her mother, would open presents 'round the tree on Christmas morning: a radio-controlled model airplane for Gabe, a new doll for Sammy, an antique pipe rack for Howard, and, for me, an atomizer of some more mature scent than the youthful Fracas which, as a wife and mother, I had outgrown—perhaps Chanel No. 5 or Joy by Jean Patou.

But it was not to be! It could *never be*, unless somehow I could find a way to meet my future husband. We were meant to be together. I knew it in the very marrow of my bones, and yet a whole year had passed and I had nothing to show for it other than a few of his pubic hairs that I had taken from a bar of soap in the men's locker room at the swimming pool late one night following water polo practice.*

Howard would be a senior that fall. I had just nine months remaining in which to act. I had to splash some cold water on my face, toss those fashion magazines in the trash, and stop feeling sorry for myself. I had to get serious about making Howard Biddle my

---

* At least, I believed them to be his and treated them as though they were. But looking back all these years later, I wonder if perhaps they might have been someone else's and whether the little shrine I built was not to Howard's pubic hair after all but rather to some complete stranger's.

boyfriend and eventual husband and stop pussy-footing around. No more sneaking around in the bushes, hiding in men's bathroom stalls, and putting masking tape over door bolts to keep them from locking automatically behind me. Selina the Sophomore was going to take the direct approach.

And so it was that I returned to Smith and Hubbard House that fall with a newfound sense of purpose. Wendy and I were now sharing a double room, since Barbara had opted not to return to college.*

No sooner had I returned to campus than I received a blow that sent me reeling. Howard Biddle had a girlfriend. Let that sink in. Howard. Biddle. Had. A. Girlfriend. The word had spread through Northampton like wildfire. Howard was going steady with Sarah Monroe, a senior at Smith and the captain of the tennis team. Sarah was tall, she was beautiful, she was rich, she was nice. I think I cried

---

* And thereby hangs a somewhat cautionary tale: Although we had never really bonded across the vast social and economic gulf that separated us, Barbara had proved to be a good freshman roommate in one particular respect: Her older brothers were able and more than willing to obtain alcohol for us. Barbara didn't drink, but she did understand that having alcohol for parties, even when they were just hen parties, was one of the cornerstones of popularity at Smith and, I would imagine, college everywhere. I will never know how the resident proctor, a fun-hating engineering grad student from Pakistan or India or one of those places, got wind of the fact that Wendy and I were having gin and tonics with Gigi Pell, an adventurous girl who lived across the hall, in our room one Friday evening freshman year. Perhaps we were making a bit too much noise and playing Steve Winwood too loudly. In any case, when she knocked on the door, we, assuming she was cool, did not bother to hide the half-gallon of Old London Town Gin that Barbara's brother Rudy had sold us that afternoon at a 20 percent markup. Long story short, when she asked how we had obtained the liquor, Wendy and I, bound by the college's strict honor code, were forced to turn Barbara in. She was suspended as soon as she got back from the library and eventually forced to withdraw, leaving behind her completely unrealistic dreams of one day becoming a doctor.

for a week when I heard the news. My thoughts raced: What could I possibly do to make Howard fall out of love with Sarah and fall in love with me instead? I bet he wouldn't love her so much if she were in a wheelchair! But what if he did? And I had crippled her for nothing??

I couldn't think clearly. In addition to doing my homework for me, Wendy now had to attend my classes in addition to her own in order to keep up with my course load. I wandered aimlessly. Days and nights passed. Weeks, maybe. My future, the beautiful future I had planned in such painstaking detail, had vanished right before my eyes just as, I was certain, it was finally within my grasp, with just a teeny tiny bit more surveillance of Howard.

This is a dangerous thing for a politician to admit, but I have never been much of a prayer. Yes, I am a spiritual person. But, like most normal people, I find religious people super-annoying. But I was desperate. And so, I prayed.

And, one night, my prayers were answered.

It was late. I was sitting on a bench outside Comstock House, where Sarah Monroe lived, and I was thinking. Just thinking. Yes, I had some knitting needles and a small hammer with me, but those could have just been for knitting. Maybe I dozed off. I had often spent the night on that bench. It had a particularly secluded location and there was a hedge nearby—but not *too* nearby—where I could relieve myself when nature called. I was awakened by the sound of an argument coming from what I knew to be the window of Sarah's bedroom. A man and a woman were whispering with the sort of intensity that indicates that the parties are in the midst of a heated disagreement.

"You're drunk!" the woman was saying. "I've told you how unattractive you are when you're drunk."

"Come on, Annabelle, don't be like that!" the man responded in a pleading tone.

"Annabelle?! Who the f-ck is Annabelle? You know what? Get the f-ck out of here! I always thought you were kind of gross anyway."

"I love you! I love you!" And then the man began weeping.

Somewhere a door slammed. And then, a moment later, framed in the light of the open door to the outside, there *he* was. Howard Biddle. The man of my dreams. He was swaying gently from side to side like a stately oak in the breeze. He must have been asleep at Sarah's and was still groggy after having been awakened by the couple arguing.

He hesitated at the top of a small staircase and I rushed over to him. "Here," I said. "Let me help."

As it turned out, Howard and I did not end up having much of a romance. We spent that first night together after I had roused Wendy and asked her to sleep at the student union, and then he would return every so often, usually late in the evening, drawn, as it were, like a moth to a flame. He would throw handfuls of gravel at my window or just shout until I came down to let him in. It was beautiful and pure and very special in a way. Yes, I cried and pleaded and begged for more—what woman wouldn't? But I also slept soundly in his arms, soothed by the sweet lullaby of his snores every few weeks and that, surely, was something I had and no one else did.

The word "sophomore" is derived from the Ancient Greek words for "knowing" and "more." Your average college sophomore, whether today, or when I was in college, or back in Ancient Greece, thinks they know or "soph" more than they actually do. Although I was uncommonly poised for my age and wise well beyond my years, I, too, had things to learn.

Although the wild romance of my relationship with Howard brought me great joy and considerably enhanced sexual skills, it also left me with quite a bit of spare time. I knew that this was due to

Howard's respect for me and desire that I devote myself to my studies in preparation for our life together in which I would be expected to make clever and amusing conversation with his family, friends, business associates, and the international jet set. But it did also give me time to think and, in my experience, thinking is almost always bad.

And so it was that one day while I was sitting and thinking on a sunny patch of Chapin Lawn, Fate's Fickle Frisbee flew out of nowhere and struck me on the head. The flinger of said Frisbee was lean and freckled, with a tousled mane of ginger red hair that was, as my father would have said, "Much in need of the attentions of a good barber."

"Are you okay?" the redheaded boy asked. "Sorry, we're pretty baked. This Nepalese hash completely f-cks with your balance."

After standing up and dusting myself off, I assured him that I was fine and started to go. He stuck out his hand and introduced himself. "I'm Ziggy."

It turned out that his real name was Thomas Howe IV, and he was a sophomore at nearby Hampshire College, the acknowledged "bad boy" among the institutions of higher learning in the general vicinity of Smith. He was at Smith to play at a party with his Grateful Dead cover band, Eyes of the World. He invited me to come see him perform that night, and somewhat to my own surprise, I did.

All through his set, he was looking at me, smiling and laughing and singing particular lyrics, as it were, directly to me. When it came time for their finale, "Fire on the Mountain" into "Bertha" into "One More Saturday Night," he said huskily into the microphone, "This one is for pretty Selina."

Afterward, Ziggy invited me back to his friend Desi's apartment and, again surprising myself, I accepted. Now, apart from prescription sleeping pills, I have never been much of a drug person. I smoked an occasional cigarette, to be sure, partly in the belief passed down from my mother that cigarettes were slimming and that a woman's hand looked especially attractive while holding one. I had tried pot once or twice and found the experience pleasant, if unremarkable. But I was not prepared when Ziggy unwrapped a large block of greasy black hashish with "epal" stamped on it (he had already smoked the "N"), broke off a sizable lump, put it in a pipe, lit it, inhaled deeply, and then passed it to me.

The next thing I knew, bright sunlight was streaming in a window and I was lying on a futon in Desi's apartment in just my panties and an Andover T-shirt. Ziggy was next to me, and when he saw that I was awake he rolled over and stroked my cheek with the back of his hand and said, "You're beautiful, Selina. I love you."

The year I spent with Ziggy on tour with Eyes of the World was a happy one. Gone were the tensions associated with my pursuit of Howard. Ziggy was warm and loving and easygoing, and he openly worshipped me, unlike Howard's more reserved form of worshipping me. We traveled all over New England in Ziggy's Plymouth Barracuda, smoking cigarettes and singing along to Dead bootleg tapes. We smoked the "e" of the hash block, then the "p," and then the "a," and finally the "l." We smoked enormous Cheech & Chong reefers rolled from the earliest strains of sinsemilla marijuana that hippie botanists had begun growing out West. We took LSD. We ate mushrooms and vomited peyote.

I tell you all this not in the interest of making a tawdry confession but rather to make it clear that when it comes to discussing drug policy in America, I know whereof I speak (more about cocaine and crack later), and I do not judge anyone. I should stress that throughout this Bohemian phase, Wendy kept my grades up and Ziggy, who was a pure math major, remained at the top of his class, eventually graduating summa cum laude and going to work on Wall Street, where he made billions developing the complex derivative algorithms that caused the 2008 financial collapse.

In the end it was Wendy who would bring this idyllic, long, strange, but lovely trip to an abrupt end. During an extended stay back in the Northampton area for a series of gigs at Smith, Amherst, and elsewhere, I had made the colossal mistake of introducing Wendy to Buzz, who played the electric organ and sometimes the melodica in Ziggy's band. We all took a lot of acid, sure. Everybody did. But Buzz took more than the rest of us combined, and Wendy, given the weakness of her personality, proved highly susceptible to hallucinogens. One night Buzz took her to a Dead show at the Centrum in Worcester and put a small square of blotter acid decorated with a picture of Mickey Mouse on her tongue, whereupon she disappeared, only to turn up four months later pregnant with Bob Weir's baby.

I tell you these boring details to make clear the cause of the crisis that ensued. Without Wendy to handle my mundane academic chores, I was obliged to begin attending classes, reading textbooks, and writing papers, something I was never good at and for which what little skill I had had utterly atrophied. As much as I wanted to keep touring with Eyes, I was petrified of flunking out and having to return to what now seemed like the hopelessly humdrum and provincial life of the Baltimore suburbs.

But there was to be a silver lining to the dark cloud of renewed collegiate drudgery, in the person of Professor Olara Emeku.

Born Derrick Jones in Paterson, New Jersey, Professor Emeku had rebranded himself as every rich liberal's favorite Marxist intellectual, fond of quoting Burke and Hegel alongside Marcus Garvey and Malcolm X. An arrest (and eventual acquittal) for involvement in a plot to bomb the Jefferson Memorial gave him both street cred and an alluring aura of danger. Eager to lure him from Columbia, Smith had created an Institute for the Study of the Culture of Race and installed him at the head of it in addition to making him a full professor at age thirty-one. The ISCR was beloved by Smith undergraduates for its course offerings in which one was graded more for professing commitment to class struggle and decrying the thought crimes of one's own bourgeois cohort than for garden-variety academic excellence per se.

He was, to put it mildly, a superstar. And the first time I saw him, I knew I wanted to f-ck him.

In order to manage her double course load, Wendy had signed me up for Professor Emeku's History of Jazz course, primarily because it was scheduled on Saturday mornings, when few other classes were held. With my lifestyle at the time, Saturday mornings were not exactly when I was at my sharpest, and I arrived at my first class (it was officially the third class, but Wendy had attended the first two before she bailed on me) about 15 minutes late. Professor Emeku was in the middle of an extended scat performance of a Miles Davis solo from *Bitches Brew*. He stopped abruptly when I entered and coldly asked for my name. He then told me to come and speak to him during his office hours. Instead of continuing with Miles Davis, he launched into a lengthy diatribe against white entitlement, which seemed to have little to do with jazz but everything to do with me and my late entrance.

The professor's office hours were held on Saturday afternoons at his house rather than, as was customary, in his actual offices. When I got there at about 4:30, he greeted me at the door of his perfectly restored colonial rectory in the town square with two glasses of Lynch-Bages, one of his beloved expensive Bordeaux, and wearing a loose light cotton robe made from a fabric with a vaguely African pattern on it. He invited me into his cozy, book-lined study, where a fire was burning on the hearth, and then proceeded, as per my plan, to f-ck my brains out for the next eleven hours.

In the weeks that followed, Olara set about reeducating me—or, as he might have described it, "educating" me—in all manner of subjects. Given his broad-ranging intellect, some deficiency or jejune opinion of mine in one area would inevitably lead him to another area in which I would also be found lacking. Our marathon Saturday afternoon sex sessions would end with an early Sunday morning walk of shame, laden with a stack of books and a lengthy reading list.

In class he often singled me out for abuse as the embodiment of a particular sort of unconscious, patronizing prejudice masked as interest and enthusiasm that he found all around him, most especially in college towns and other liberal enclaves. We quickly discovered that the more extreme the public humiliation, the more intense our private pleasure became. Now, most former presidents probably wouldn't admit this, but when I was younger I often found being insulted and humiliated, especially when the treatment is witnessed by others, to be a potent aphrodisiac. As I have gotten older, I have found the reverse to be increasingly true: that attacking someone else, especially without justification, can often be a prelude to a deeply passionate sexual encounter. This is, I suppose, a sign of maturity.

Professor Emeku dumped me in a manner fully befitting the entire arc of our relationship: by giving me an "F" on my term paper ("Toward a Metaphysics of Subjugation: A New Synthesis"), an "F" on my final exam, and an "F" in his course. When I arrived at his office hours to ask him why, I saw, through a window, him lecturing another coed in front of the fire while wearing his tribal bathrobe. Relentless doorbell ringing and the hurling of a flower pot through the window brought nothing more than an eventual restraining order. Assuming that the restraining order was a coy effort to play hard-to-get, very much in keeping with the heretofore playful nature of our relationship, led to several arrests, which required a significant intervention on the part of my parents with the college. The Eaton Faculty Gymnasium at Smith still bears mute witness to this difficult time in my life.

After a summer spent hiking in Europe in the vicinity of a wonderful Swiss sanitarium, I returned to Smith for my senior year still somewhat adrift, feeling as though perhaps I had not accomplished as much in my first three years of college as I would have liked. I found some small measure of solace in finally applying myself to my studies and discovering, as so many had before me, that if one avoids the hard sciences, college is pretty easy.

I first met Andrew Meyer in Hasselmeyer's, a long-defunct upscale coffee shop just off campus. This was the pre-Starbucks era, a difficult time in the coffee world, as storefronts which had thrived for a generation as beatnik-style coffeehouses, began to make the painful transition to a new marketplace in which espresso and cappuccino called the tune. In some respects, establishments that catered to college students were better equipped to handle this metamorphosis than other, more mainstream coffee shops and diners, since their customers had long been on the adventurous vanguard of hot beverage consumption, beginning with the arrival of herbal teas as other than a strictly ethnic product sometime in the late '70s. College students were in the main early adopters of new types of coffee and coffee accoutrements, and in this respect I was a typical college student.

And yet, looking back, it is easy to see why Hasselmeyer's did not become Starbucks and why America is now home to tens of thousands of Starbucks franchises as opposed to tens of thousands of Hasselmeyer franchises. The problem was that Hasselmeyer's chose an Old Vienna theme that fell between the stools of the studied informality of what I will call the "Starbucks style" and the formal service of a white tablecloth restaurant. In any case, given what I have told you about Hasselmeyer's, it is easy to see how I might have found myself there on a rainy Wednesday afternoon treating myself to a piece of depression strudel and a *kaffee mit schlag* as part of the overeating therapy I had successfully employed as part of a multi-phase recovery from my badly broken heart.

Ironically, Andrew was there on a first date, though not with me. He had chosen Hasselmeyer's, he later told me, as well as the particular time of day (mid-afternoon) in a complex hedging of bets that I think illustrates the workings of Andrew's particularly brilliant mind. On the one hand, he wanted to impress a girl he had been told was sophisticated and intelligent—though to me she looked like the standard hairy-armpitted poetry magazine assistant editor type—but didn't want to spend too much money. If one ordered carefully, Hasselemeyer's seemed more expensive than it actually was, and the waiters in their black vests and bow ties and floor-length white aprons tied around their waists added a note of Old World je ne sais quoi. The afternoon menu also consisted mostly of pastries and some small salads, as opposed to the far more costly goulashes and *Wiener schnitzels* that became available after 6 P.M. If, Andrew had reasoned, he liked the girl and felt her worth the investment, he could ask her to stay for dinner. If not, he could cut his losses with a *café liégeois* and some profiteroles.

As things turned out, she didn't even get those.

Andrew and the girl, we'll call her "Deirdre" since that was her name, were seated a few tables away from me. The restaurant was mostly unoccupied, in a foreshadowing of its imminent failure and indeed the impending discrediting of the entire Hasselmeyer's concept. As soon as he sat down, Andrew began stealing glances at me, which soon turned into brazen staring as his date droned on about this or that. Before she could even order, he stood up, came over to me, and asked if the extra chair at my table was taken. I told him that it wasn't and that he could take it but was surprised when, instead of taking it over to his table, he sat down at mine. I must have looked confused, because he quickly explained that he had made a mistake in asking the other girl out because she was boring him and he liked me more. When, after a moment, she came over to ask him what was going on, he told her the exact same thing.

Deirdre left in tears, which we both agreed was unfortunate and we wish hadn't happened but also that she was at least partly to blame because she had not made more of an effort to be amusing and appealing. That got us talking, and soon we were laughing and the next thing you know we were dating.

My father never much liked Andrew. No doubt Andrew got off on the wrong foot by asking my father to invest in some scheme of his before my father could ask Andrew the same thing. But my mother always liked him, if only for the very obvious flattery that he showered upon her. Andrew always brought flowers and always told her she looked as though she had lost weight and that he loved her new hairstyle. He never became fully integrated into my social circle, but he mixed well with both the country club crowd and the working stiffs, even if his small talk always remained very small.

The one thing Andrew had that really drew me to him was a simmering ambition both for himself and for me. He always believed, from the beginning, that I could do great things and that one of his duties as a boyfriend, and eventually my husband, was to keep me motivated and focused. It was Andrew who suggested that I apply to law school—and not just any law school, but to Yale Law School, then, as now, considered to be one of the nation's finest. He coached me through my LSATs, edited and reedited my application, and strategized endlessly about which of my parents' friends to enlist to write letters. In the end, whatever he did worked, and I was admitted, but to this day I still believe that Andrew could have become a brilliant lawyer himself if he had devoted as much energy to practicing the law as he did to evading it.

That fall we moved into an apartment in a house in a somewhat sketchy neighborhood in New Haven (where virtually every neighborhood is somewhat sketchy). I studied and attended classes while Andrew attempted to get his restaurant delivery business off the ground. His company, 2 Good 2 Go, was a forerunner of Postmates and Uber Eats and other delivery services and really seemed for a while like it was going to succeed. It really did.

This was the first time in my life when I had lived with a boyfriend and, to put it mildly, it took some getting used to. Neither of us are what you would call "neatniks" or even "neat." This is not to say that we liked living in mess and squalor; neither of us wanted that, either. We both just wanted the other to clean. Andrew felt I should do it because I was a woman, and I felt he should do it since he made most of the mess and seemed to have a great deal of free time. In the end, the solution was so obvious that afterward we both wondered why we had not seen it sooner. We hired Maria, a hard-working immigrant from somewhere in Latin America, to come in three times a week and clean and prepare our dinners in advance. I have always believed that immigration is the lifeblood of our country, and it was deeply satisfying to put those beliefs into practice.

The three years at Yale flew by as I learned the law and Andrew honed his skill for business by starting one company after another. Although some of the passion between us had faded into comfortable domesticity, we were generally happy together, and I discovered that by applying the energy and ingenuity I had devoted to hopeless relationships to my studies, I actually could learn something. Warm and nurturing at home, Andrew retained his gregarious manner outside the house, and the large number of female undergraduates he employed for his business ventures—which seemed unable to support a payroll of more than one and maybe not even that—was the only recurrent source of tension in our relationship.

Despite those few rocky moments, graduation day 1989 found us still together and pondering our next move as I received my diploma with my father looking on proudly while Andrew flirted with my mother.

CHAPTER FIVE

Adventures in the Private Sector

A frequent criticism of people who work in government is that they lack experience in the real world and, detached from any connection with the daily lives of ordinary citizens, they are unable to effectively address their needs and wants. I bet there's an old joke or two about this. How many times have you read about some government initiative—a new bridge, a new food stamp program, a new war—and said to yourself, "Why the h-ll is the government doing that with my money?! I don't want that!" In fact, it's often hard to think of anything that the government *does* do that people really like, other than giving them free money in various forms. The counterargument that is often made, along the lines of, "Hey, that road you drove on today when you went to the liquor store? Do you know who built that? That's right! The government!" just gets on people's nerves, and they either respond by saying, "F-ck that! I didn't ask the government to build a road. I'd be perfectly happy walking to the liquor store on a dirt road or by cutting my way through a dense forest, if necessary. A person who goes to the liquor store as much as I do probably shouldn't be driving anyway!" or by deciding that you're the kind of as-h-ole or d-ck that no one likes because you're constantly saying dumb, aggravating sh-t like this.

If you've been in the government or really in any kind of respon-sible position, you know that people are never going to be grateful to you for all the hard work and sacrifices you make. It's human nature to be ungrateful. Every woman knows a little bit about the author Ayn Rand that she learned from the worst boyfriend she ever had. And while Rand's books are nothing more than bound j-zz rags for involuntarily celibate adolescents of any age, she was right about people being fundamentally selfish. So, no matter what you do in gov-ernment, people aren't going to like it much, and that's why, if you're the sort of needy person who requires constant favorable attention and approval from others, you should probably go into some other line of work. Still, you can avoid at least some of the attacks by hav-ing spent a little time working in the private sector. Ideally, you would have risen to some position of responsibility so that you can tell the voters that you "know what it means to make a payroll" or "build a business" or some other kind of foolishness. Believe it or not, there are still lots of people out there who think government should be "run like a business," although the kind of business they seem to have in mind is a big box store with extra-large shopping carts that turns a blind eye toward shoplifters.

On the rare occasion when something genuinely surprising hap-pens in politics, journalists and pundits are quick to fall back on the idea that someone has figured out some new way to scratch the innu-merable itches (not to mention chronic pustulent sores) of a group of supposedly "forgotten" Americans. The truth—and I'm going to give it to you straight here—is that they've found some convincing way to promise our most worthless citizens that they will get something— probably electronics of some type, most often video games—without having to work for it. I know that may sound racist. I wish it were that simple. But the fact is that 100 percent of Americans consider themselves "forgotten" and, I've found, candidates are successful or not depending on how much they "remember" to promise things to the most gullible of these people while "forgetting" to ask them for anything in return.

But, look, I don't want to get sidetracked.

My point is that lots of people will attribute magical powers to business experience even when they've worked in a business or even owned one and should know better. But complaining about how stupid voters are never gets a politician anywhere.

At the time that I embarked upon the world as a newly minted law school graduate, I was not yet thinking of running for office. So I did not assign any particular value to one type of job over another as far as its potential future appeal to American voters. Knowing what I know now, if I had to go back and do it all again, I'd probably have tried to work for at least a few weeks at some sort of demeaning-but-not-too-demeaning job so that I could frame my life story as a classic American success story. Since my first run for office, I've claimed to have "put myself through law school," which I honestly believe is technically true. I mean who else put me through it? Yes, my mother paid the tuition and gave me an inadequate allowance but, unlike in college, *I* was the one doing all the work, by attending classes and reading books and writing papers and other law school things.

But, having put myself through law school, it was not like I was going to work as a stevedore or in a slaughterhouse, and so I never had the chance to put one of those colorful, supposedly character-building menial occupations on my resume. For a lawyer, the equivalent is to go to work as a public defender or for some kind of activist group that wastes everyone's time by harassing businesses or the government. Whenever you hear someone say they are an "environmental lawyer" or a "civil rights lawyer," watch out! These are generally either people who couldn't get hired at a decent law firm or people who always had their eye on running for office and just pretended to be lawyers for a while. The only thing worse is an "international lawyer," which even international lawyers have trouble saying with a straight face.

I suppose working as a prosecutor or district attorney is a little above the slaughterhouse level. It looks good on a politician's CV, plus it can maybe be a little interesting sometimes and maybe even a bit exciting if you get to put someone in jail or the gas chamber. Or so you might think. But I've met a few prosecutors and district attorneys in my time, and when you get a few drinks into them (never hard!), they'll tell you that it's a lot of work for not much reward and then start talking smack about how feeble public defenders and Legal Aid types are. One thing you can never forget is that everyone likes to have someone else to look down on.

As it turned out, I didn't spend a great many years in the world of corporate law, but the time I did spend was formative and constructive. A foundation in the law is, I believe, a useful thing for almost any politician, and the ones who come from other fields of endeavor like academia, the clergy, or medicine are always looked at askance and, often, with derision. The ones who come from business are even more dubious, since it can be surprisingly hard to tell if they're actually worth the hundreds of millions of dollars they claim or are secretly broke. I learned from painful experience that anyone who calls himself a "successful businessman" without providing real concrete verifiable details (e.g., "I'm the president of Google. You can Google it.") is actually a charlatan. Voters, the poor fools, are rarely clever enough to figure this out.

Still, although I have always been mature for my age, like many young people fresh out of school, I wanted to see a bit of what the world had to offer before settling on a lifetime profession. Some young people do this by joining the Peace Corps or by sampling the worlds of art or fashion. So many of them waste time in the world of being unsuccessful actors that you almost wouldn't believe it. (My daughter actually explored the world of performance art, thereby becoming one of the first people to figure out how to dance naked in front of a bunch of leering men without getting paid for it.) In my case, the world I was interested in exploring was the world of corporate law.

There are almost as many different kinds of corporate law as there are corporations, and there are other kinds of law, such as trusts and estates or white-collar criminal defense, that are often handled by corporate law firms even though they don't necessarily involve corporations directly. One of the things that appealed to me the most about the venerable firm of Maltby, Pierpont, and Blumfeld, where I accepted a job as a junior associate after interviewing at a number of competitors, was the opportunity to work for a month in each of the firm's specialty practices. Not all of the other firms were able to offer this sort of enticement or, if they did, they didn't offer it to me since they didn't offer me a job. But though perhaps not among the top tier firms, which, back in 1994 were still closed to women except for a certain "type" of woman, Maltby, Pierpont, and Blumfeld was perfectly respectable and, I thought, a good fit for a young lawyer like me who wanted to work hard but not too hard and have a social life and go to the gym. The fact that my mother's first cousin, my "Uncle" (as I called him) George was a partner and that the firm managed her trust also suggested that Maltby, Pierpont, and Blumfeld was the sort of place where I might fit in and where the other lawyers would be predisposed to see my value.

As I moved around the firm getting practical hands-on experience in dealing with clients such as insurance companies and reinsurance companies, I quickly determined which areas of the law I liked and which I did not. As any lawyer will tell you, many areas of the law are, quite honestly, really idiotic. I had decided on my first day of work that, in order to make my mark, I would never compromise my core value of plainspoken honesty. So as I moved through the first-year associates' cycle from department to department, I tried in the course of the daily grind to take a moment to stop and carefully listen to myself. Was I enjoying the work I was doing? Was it stimulating? Was I learning anything? I shared my answers to these questions with my superiors, judging that they, too, would wish to constantly reassess the work they were doing and whether it was really worthwhile, as well as their own performance. I had thought that this kind of back-and-forth, give-and-take approach would be something that the law firm as an institution would also support, since the bedrock of the law itself is the principle of giving due weight to alternative viewpoints.

And yet here as so often before and after, I found myself stymied by patriarchal prejudice, with my co-workers stubbornly unwilling to listen to my constructive criticism or overall evaluations. By observing their behavior, I became versed in certain commonplace tactics for delay and buck passing. They would pretend to be interested in what I was saying and then ask me to put my thoughts in writing, or they would begin to cross-examine me about what exactly I found boring about, say, tax practice or maritime law, as though I were some sort of a hostile witness. After a few months of this, it became clear to me that I was wasting my time as a junior associate, and the path that lay ahead toward partnership seemed impossibly long and by no means certain.

The lack of enthusiasm on the part of my bosses for my suggestions might have discouraged a weaker personality, but I resolved that I would never give up fighting the wrongs I encountered in life, whether they concerned the civil rights of under-enfranchised minority groups or aspects of the practice of law that are just extremely picky and dull. For their part, my bosses often found it easier to give me time off than to risk being shown up by a "mere woman." Fine. So be it. I would use the extra free time to improve myself in other ways and gain a wider experience of the world.

As I endured those difficult years at Maltby, Pierpont, and Blumfeld (along with a delightful interlude in Europe about which you'll read more later. I could have included it here, but I want to give you an incentive to keep reading), I was also enduring the rigors of daily living. My modest salary and Andrew's sporadic income imposed upon us a humble existence, living in an unused wing of my mother's house and obliged to depend upon her servants for meals, laundry, and house-keeping because we could not afford to set up a household on our own. While my relationship with my mother has always been strained, I think Andrew found this time especially hard, since it offended his macho pride not to be able to support me better. Most of the income we did have was invested in his various businesses and at least one invention for finding water using a radically improved dowsing rod, and, as he explained to me, the payoff might be far in the distance. However, there were at least a few times when the possible future payoff seemed to recede so far into the distance as to be altogether invisible, like when one of his businesses would collapse completely, leaving angry creditors in a much better position to recover any future payoff than I.

It was after one of the more spectacular of Andrew's business fail-ures, a system for franchising the door-to-door sales of poor-quality sporting goods manufactured in Vietnam, that Andrew asked me to marry him. In retrospect, his error had been a rather obvious one.

Since no one in Vietnam played football or baseball or hockey, it was understandable, I suppose, that they might not have understood exactly the nature of the equipment required. Plus, their manufacturing techniques, which Andrew had promoted as "traditional" and "handmade," resulted in an entire order of footballs being made from the skin of the pig's face, which was the cheapest pig leather one could buy and hence offered the greatest profit margin. The moment when Andrew took delivery of the six thousand footballs with pig snouts and eye sockets clearly visible on them was, I think, the saddest I had ever seen him. Broke, exhausted, and weeping, he fell on his knees and asked me to marry him.

I said yes.

CHAPTER SIX

Climbing Capitol Hill—
A Woman in the House . . . and the Senate

Congress, like life, has two halves, and it has been my honor to serve in both of them.

First, the House of Representatives.

When I reflect upon the many difficult decisions I have made in my time on the blue marble we call planet Earth—the decision, for example, to devote my life to standing up against injustice on behalf of ordinary, decent people, or my six abortions—one decision takes pride of place as not only difficult but crucially important in defining both my personal history and also the history of our great nation, the United States of America.

As I think back upon my time honorably serving the people of Maryland's 14th District (formerly the 22nd District, now eliminated following a census fraud investigation) in the United States House of Representatives, the memories are overwhelming. They appear as a jumbled kaleidoscope of images, many of them crystal clear, others faded with time, some to such an extent that they are now merely partial recollections for which I do not believe I can be sued for libel, since I am not asserting them as facts but rather as things that *might* have happened. It would be best, I think, for both myself, my aide Mike

McLintock, who assisted me in researching this book, and my readers to take what I am about to tell you here and elsewhere in that spirit.

The year was 1996. Andrew and I, still comparative newlyweds, were living outside Baltimore while I took a break from my thriving law practice in order to have a baby and Andrew was busy building the ninth or tenth of his many businesses, in this case selling a proprietary technology that allowed users to inject powdered ink into used printer cartridges to prolong their life indefinitely. The product relied on acquiring—in bulk and at a steep discount—syringes that, though perfectly functional, were defective in some minor way so that they could not be used on people.

Andrew is one of those rare individuals who sees opportunities where others see only vulnerabilities. His is a sort of restless intelligence that moves lightning fast from project to project and vulnerability to opportunity. Like so many young people, Andrew and I saw the world as our oyster. For me, the pearl awaiting inside the moist, gray flesh with a faintly mushroom-like aroma was high political office; for Andrew it was the invisible beauty of market efficiencies.

Life, however, as they say, "comes at you," and, sure enough, just when we seemed to have settled into a comfortable routine and despite many layers of precaution, I became pregnant.

I recall lying there in the hospital with my newborn daughter screaming and clawing at my chest like the title character in the movie *Alien* and thinking, "Is this all there is? What's next? What's next for Selina Meyer?" I resolved right then and there that I would run for Congress and begin the next chapter of my life. I had been many things already: daughter, student, graduate student, lawyer, wife, mother . . . and I had succeeded brilliantly at all of them. But it is in my nature to always strive for more, to look beyond the nearest horizon to the one farther away, and then the one beyond that.

And so, my irrepressible spirit sought a new challenge and, sure enough, found one. As is so often the case in life, this new opportunity was right outside my front door, staring me, as it were, in the face. And though some might have deemed it Quixotic, for me the question was not "Can I do it?" but rather "How can I live with myself if I do not?"

Conrad Boyle had represented the 14th Congressional District of Maryland for thirty-two terms and was now approaching his ninetieth year. While many of Conrad's supporters insisted that he had not lost a step, there were others—though out of respect for his long service they were not vocal about it—who felt otherwise. During his final two decades in the House, he had become known for highly eccentric interrogations of witnesses during Congressional hearings, principally on personal issues such as how much they weighed (he believed that he could reliably guess someone's weight to within a pound), what sort of car they drove, and the names of their pets. He would claim that these seemingly unrelated details could help him determine if the witnesses were telling the truth or, in the case of nominees for political office, whether they were suited to be undersecretaries or ambassadors. But after a time, his colleagues on both sides of the aisle wearied of Boyle's hectoring, feeling that he tended to derail the momentum of hearings with his bizarre lines of questioning.

Though many believed it was time for him to go, no one seemed willing to make a decisive move against a legislator with Boyle's seniority—especially one who had served as a Navy cook in the Aleutian Islands during World War II and was always ready to roll up his pant leg to show off the scar from an war wound he had received while attempting to use a cooking pot as a kind of a water ski—and so it was that he died in the midst of an extended and rather heated discussion with a nominee for a federal judgeship about two dogs he owned that, despite being different breeds, had very similar names.

With Election Day just weeks away, there was an immediate mad scramble to succeed Congressman Boyle. The oddsmakers predicted that either Boyle's wife or son would inherit his seat, but since the son was in his mid-seventies and his wife was in her early twenties, age was an issue for both potential candidates.

The first step in any campaign is to put together a team of "wise men" (or women!) to serve as counselors and also, one hopes, donors. For advice, I turned first to my "rabbi," the senior partner in my law firm, Abe Blumfeld. As always, Abe was refreshingly candid. He told me that while he would be more than happy to arrange a leave of absence for me from the law firm, he did not think I had what he called a "Chinaman's Chance" of winning in the primary, much less the general election. "Bubbeleh," he said, "Come and sit on my lap." After I had settled myself, he went on, "Those *goyische* schmucks want a mensch to vote for, someone they can have a beer with. You, you're like a little china doll. Have you seen the women who go into politics?" And then he spat. "They're like dogs! Disgusting, every single one of them. They look like they smell! What's this?" This last question was in reference to a roll of postpartum fat on my stomach that he was pinching.

As I left Abe's office, I faced my first real moment of doubt. Was I simply too attractive for politics? Abe had declined to make a campaign contribution, saying that he was giving me something even more precious: good advice. But as we all know, campaigns run on money the way cars run on gasoline. Good advice is more like windshield-wiper fluid or maybe that deodorizing liquid that you sometimes see on the dashboard in taxis. Facing this stern reality, after addressing my primary responsibility by hiring a wonderful caregiver, Inez or, maybe, Carmen, for my baby, who was proving to be quite a handful already, I began what would become the familiar routine of pounding the pavement asking for money.

For the next seven months, I knocked on hundreds of doors, made thousands of phone calls, and sat on countless laps. If I had ever had any fear of rejection, I learned to get over it in a hurry. I also quickly came to appreciate the truth of what Abe had told me about the voters' need to relate to politicians both as ordinary "people like them" and as godlike superhumans—haughty and beautiful and with an unconcealed disdain for people whom they viewed as "not as good" as they were, which was pretty much everyone.

I had the second part down. But I struggled to "relate" to people who were so different from those I had grown up with, gone to college with, raced yachts against, and come out with at debutante parties. First of all, there was the problem of their ugly houses with weird smells and their terrible taste in décor, clothing, and hairstyles. Campaigning door to door was truly an eye-opening experience, or really more often an "eye-closing" experience for me because that is usually what I wanted to do as soon as I got a peek inside the front door: close my eyes.

There are, as I rapidly learned, a few simple tricks for successful campaigning. The easiest one is to replace the word "horrible" with the word "delicious." For example, if you feel an impulse to exclaim, "Good Lord, what a horrible smell!" you instead say, "Good Lord, what a delicious smell!" If you, being perhaps a more subtle, interrogative type of person, feel inclined to ask, "Oh, my God, what is that horrible smell?" you instead ask, "Oh, my God, what is that delicious smell?" It even sometimes works for non-olfactory issues, as in "Look at those *delicious* children!" or "I can truly say that I cannot recall when I have had a more *delicious* experience."

The problem with the horrible/delicious switcheroo (and also why I don't mind telling you about it, even though you might be inclined to steal it to use yourself), is that sometimes when you tell someone that their cooking smells delicious, they will offer you some of whatever they are cooking. And then you'll really be up a certain well-known creek. In those cases, there is only one recourse: to claim to be allergic to whatever is being cooked. To this day, on certain blocks in Baltimore, I am known in one house as "the lady who is allergic to stew" and right next door as "the lady who is allergic to our national dish made from rotten seafood."

Funny story: While a conversation about food and cooking may seem like a good ice-breaker with the kind of people who can't afford to go to restaurants, there are times when it has the opposite effect. Back in those pre–crystal meth days, in certain neighborhoods, sometimes what was cooking wasn't even food at all, but rather crack cocaine.

Although it has since faded from popularity, crack cocaine* was once all the rage, especially in places like inner-city Baltimore, part of which lay in my district. By way of a quick refresher, I should explain that to make crack cocaine, you mix powder cocaine with water and a base such as ammonium bicarbonate, ammonium carbonate, or, most typically because it is so readily available, sodium bicarbonate, which is otherwise known as baking soda. When heated, the mixture liquifies with the freebase cocaine forming an oily layer on top. The layer can be skimmed off and, once cooled and dried, it

* Also known as atari, base, bazooka, beamers, beemers, bebe, bee-bee, berry, bing, bolo, bomb, boulder, boulders, butter, caine, cane, Casper, Casper the ghost, cavvy, chemical, chewies, cloud, cloud nine, crills, crunch and munch, dip, famous dimes, fan, fish scale, fries, fry, glo, golfball, gravel, grit, hail, hamburger helper, hubba, ice cube, kangaroo, kibbles and bits, kibbles, krills, lightem, paste, patico, pebbles, pee wee, pony, raw, ready, ready rocks, redi rocks, roca, rock, rooster, rox, Roxanne, scud, Scotty, scramble, scruples, seven-up, sherm, sherms, sleet, snowballs, stones, teeth, tension, top gun, tweak, ultimate, wash, white cloud, work, yahoo, yay, yayoo, yeah-O, yeyo, yeo, and yuc.

can be rolled into a crack cocaine "rock" that has the appearance and consistency of hard plastic.

The great advantage of crack over powder cocaine is that the drugs reach the bloodstream faster when smoked than snorted, as powder cocaine is. The addition of the baking powder and the cooking process also serve to increase the potency and purity of the drug, and some believe that it also acts as a sort of "Hamburger Helper" by turning a small amount of powder cocaine into a rather larger amount of "rock."

The downside of crack cocaine, of course, is that cooking it can be a very smelly process indeed and that, while the smell is sharp and pungent, it does not really resemble a cooking odor but rather that of a dry-cleaning shop with very poor ventilation. I'm sure many readers are already a bit ahead of me in seeing the problem that this created for me as a novice campaigner. Having made my "horrible/delicious" substitution process second nature—almost a reflex—I would sometimes impulsively tell voters who were cooking crack and not food that I thought it smelled "delicious," which they would understandably think was a rather broad hint that I wanted some.

I have never been one to judge others, so I will simply say that I've never developed much of a taste for crack, but if others have, well, more power to them. But after offering my standard demurrer I quickly became known in certain households and crack dens as "the woman who is allergic to crack."

There were many times in that first campaign when it seemed like we were barely managing to keep our heads above water. Despite a tremendous effort on my part, we still had not managed to raise much money outside of the crack-dealing community, which had adopted me as a sort of pet. What money we did raise was quickly consumed by our expenses. My husband, Andrew, bought an Alfa Romeo sports car that he thought would save us time and enable us to make more campaign stops by virtue of its speed and maneuverability. Unfortunately, it proved to be a delicate machine, and Andrew was often away coping with the latest breakdown. Also, since it was a two-seater, even on the rare occasions it was working, the rest of my team was obliged to follow in Mike McLintock's 1977 Chevy Caprice station wagon, which he had purchased in college.

Mike loved that darn car.

They say that there are as many different kinds of love as there are words for love: adore . . . and others. Mike loved that station wagon the way you can love an ugly dog or a wayward child. He loved it for its virtues, sure: It was reliable, the backseats folded down to create enough space to carry an adult's bicycle, and it had a working cigarette lighter. But he also loved it for its flaws: It was unreliable, it would not start on especially cold days or especially warm days, and a previous owner had spilled a large quantity of milk in it, which had soaked into the carpet under one of the seats with predictable consequences.

At American University, Mike had been what's known as a "joiner," participating in intramural sports teams, social service organizations, and as many religious groups as there are religions. A strapping six-footer with a full head of ginger-red hair, Mike was regarded by men and women alike as a person of exceptional charm. Though not conventionally handsome, his warm and sensitive manner and a genuine interest in others won him countless friends and, by his senior year, the exalted post of class secretary, charged with recording the official minutes at meetings of the class president, vice president, and other officers.

It was through this early experience in college government that Mike caught the "politics bug." When he learned through a friend that

Selina Meyer was looking for a real go-getter to join her communications team, he jumped at the opportunity even though, because it was an unpaid position, he was forced to continue working at his temporary job as a short-order cook at Bubba's Subs, a popular local sandwich shop. Though he found holding down both positions exhausting, he had negotiated a sweet deal with Amir, Bubba's owner, to use the storeroom as a makeshift residence of sorts in exchange for ten additional hours of unpaid work every week. By putting a camp bed between two shelves laden with large cans, bottles, and boxes of condiments (the actual primary ingredients for the sandwiches, mainly cold cuts of different types, were stored in a large walk-in refrigerator that would have been dangerous to sleep in though arguably much quieter), I was able to make for myself a cozy redoubt, a word the meaning of which I have never entirely understood and still don't to this very day.

Did you ever notice how you always wind up giving those great old cars you love a special name? A blue car might be "Bluey," a brown car might be "Brownie" or "Brown Car." While Mike never actually got around to naming his station wagon before the malfunctioning cigarette lighter caused it to burst into flames, it was very much the sort of car you would give a name to, if that gives you any idea of the kind of car it was.

Although my many years in politics have been by and large a blessing, I would be doing a disservice both to the reading public (though the reading public and other egghead types have often disappointed me on Election Day) and posterity if I did not concede that there have occasionally been dark clouds surrounding some of the silver linings. The most persistent and most damaging of these are sexism and misogyny. While I was aware, of course, that these things existed, I had largely been spared the full brunt of them in my legal career, where many of my co-workers treated me much like Abe Blumfeld did—as a beautiful and delicate china doll to be nurtured and stroked and hugged and cuddled, not in any way abused or taken advantage of. Sure, call it sexist if you like (my male colleagues only rarely got compliments on their legs, breasts, or rear ends) but it was the kind and gentle sexism of bygone days that I think most women, even, you know, certain annoying "modern" types, would find flattering and even nurturing.

But during that first campaign, I was to learn that sexism can sometimes have a dark side. In my case, this came in the form of the vicious smear tactics that my opponent, Porter Marshall, leveled against me. He began by attacking my summa cum laude degree from Smith, claiming that, instead, I had not actually graduated from Smith because I still owed a paper or two and that, had I graduated, it certainly would not have been with honors of any kind. He went on to cast aspersions on my law degree by pointing out that since I hadn't actually graduated from Smith, I must have lied on my law school application. He told people that, contrary to what was asserted in my official biography, instead of being on the law review at Yale Law School, I had, in fact, not been on the law review. He threw everything but the kitchen sink at me, using all the ugly little tricks men have employed for centuries to keep women down. He crowed about my having had to take the bar exam so many times, on how few actual clients I had and how rarely I had prevailed in court, and most underhanded of all, he convinced the *Baltimore Sun* to run an article about my DUIs and featuring a very unflattering mug shot.[*]

The fact that everything he was saying was true did not make it any less disgusting, any less insulting, and any less an affront to the

---

[*] Just to be clear, Marshall wasn't saying or doing any of these things *personally* but there is no doubt in my mind that he was behind it all.

standards of dignity and civilized discourse that have been a hall-mark of American political engagement ever since that overrated play about how Burr shot Hamilton first premiered on Broadway. This double standard worked against me. If a man had been running and his opponent brought up his DUIs, it would have counted as a positive, especially if the candidate was a Kennedy. But in my case, people were all "women can't hold their liquor" and "women are so much less attractive than men when they're drunk."*

To say that this first bruising encounter with the proverbial "Old Boys' Club" was a wake-up call would be an understatement. Andrew, chivalrous as always, wanted to hunt Porter Marshall down and, in his words, "punch him in that stupid matinee-idol handsome face of his" and "punch his f-cking face" and "punch that f-cking guy." Andrew never got the opportunity but I, too, resolved to fight back. In politics one is constantly faced with the difficult choice of whether to take the high road or the low road. Sadly, as our political norms have collapsed and the discourse has coarsened thanks to that Hamilton play, many politicians have fought their campaigns in the mud of the low road, and it is hard not to believe that, as a society, we are very much the poorer for it.

At first glance, there were no visible chinks in Marshall's armor. A self-made multimillionaire who had married his high school sweet-heart while he was working his way through college on a football scholarship and now had a picture-perfect family with three children, one of whom had special needs (which is solid gold from a political standpoint. My daughter, Catherine, had many many special needs, especially a need for attention, but none of her needs were "special"

---

* I happen to agree with the second one but that doesn't make it any less hurtful—in fact it makes it somewhat more so.

in the special way that helps a candidate, which is just so typical of her), Marshall was poised and personable. He was also a veteran who had received the Silver Star for bravery, was a regular churchgoer who taught Sunday School, and had devoted countless hours to the community through various good works and acts of selfless public service. Plus, he had built a dozen orphanages in Haiti, one of which, Grace de Dieu Children's Home in Carrefour, had won "Orphanage of the Year" for three years running at the annual Haitian Orphanage Awards, or "Haities," as they are known. And he had graduated first in his class from Harvard Law School where, unlike me, he had also been the for-real editor of the law review. We had hoped that he had made the law review thing up like I had, but we checked and he had in fact been the editor. And he was a teetotaler. We tried attacking him on the grounds that this made him boring and not the kind of person you would like to "have a beer with" because, since he didn't drink beer, you would be having a beer by yourself while he drank some Gatorade or maybe an Arnold Palmer, which is half lemonade and half iced tea. But no sale. Moreover, he had two decades of experience as a special aide to the governor, where he had worked with governors of both parties to make government run more smoothly and be more responsive to the needs of Maryland's citizens. In this capacity, he had balanced the state budget and created a business-friendly environment that caused Maryland's economy to grow by a remarkable 15 percent per annum on average, all while expanding social services. For this work, he had accepted a token salary of $1 a year, which he made a little show of donating to the United Way. What's more, he had three rescue dogs, all extremely friendly golden retrievers that he brought with him on all his campaign appearances. I had a dog, too, but mine was a purebred shih tzu, Charlie Chan Chinky Chinky Chinaman, or "Charlie" as we called him, and we found that, despite having won Best of Breed at the Westminster Kennel Club Dog Show earlier that year, Charlie did not take readily to the campaign trail, snarling and biting passers-by, especially children in strollers. To this day, I refuse to believe that Charlie did not like children. I am certain that it was the noisy, rolling, sometimes rusty strollers that scared him and, for that, who can blame him?

I won't lie to you. The fruitless quest to find ways to attack Porter Marshall was one of the most frustrating episodes in my early political career. For the life of us, we could not find any mud to throw at the guy, and if we had found any, we weren't at all sure it would stick.

And then along came Rod Longpole.

I'm not sure how Andrew first found him, but the adult male film star Rob Longpole could have been Porter Marshall's twin brother. Tall, handsome, muscular, African-American, and exceptionally well-endowed, he was the virtual spitting image of my opponent. But *unlike* my opponent, there were hundreds of hours of video footage of Rod Longpole engaging in every imaginable homosexual sex act—plus a few that I had never imagined—with dozens of male partners, many with very bizarre and unconvincing frosted dye jobs and tattoos that made them look like a seventh grader's doodle pad. Andrew, assisted by other members of the team, scoured the entire internet—not simply PornHub and YouPorn but also RedZone, Brazzers, Men.com, Manbone, Jackbuddies, Digital Playground, Gay-but-Straight, Straight-but-Gay, Manpussylovers, and even the darkest and scariest corners of the Dark Web—and screened every single film that Rod Longpole (or Peter Rodman, as he sometimes called himself) had ever made. Andrew then put together a "best of" compilation tape, spending hours in a darkened editing room, watching facial cum shot after facial cum shot and rim job after rim job, that showed Rod having sex with dozens of men, some of them in military uniforms. It was, dare I say, a work of art as well as political paydirt. But, having watched the footage and made the tape, the next step was less clear. How could we get the tape into the hands of the people who might be disinclined to vote for a gay porn star without leaving our fingerprints all over it?

And here we made a rookie mistake.

Back in 1998 social media was still in its comparative infancy if it existed at all, and the exact mechanics of how it worked were poorly understood. In those days, the only thing that was "going viral" was the deadly AIDS virus. So when Andrew sent his porn tape to a local newspaper, he didn't realize that some basic sleuthing would allow a reporter to trace it back to our campaign. In retrospect, it would have been better to try and get the tape circulating among local high school students who have always loved that kind of thing. As it turned out, we pretty much handed the local media a negative story about ourselves, and Marshall, with his Teflon armor fully intact, wound up not even having to acknowledge all the disgusting behavior his look-alike had engaged in.

There is a footnote to the story, which is that Rod Longpole himself (real name: Franz Feldschmitt) came forward and endorsed me, saying that, thanks to Andrew's compilation tape, he had become the fifteenth most searched-for porn star on the web, up from the 27,222nd just the week before.

And so we limped into Election Day, bruised and battered, definitely older, hopefully wiser. Andrew and I voted in the basement in the Presbyterian Church with Catherine in my arms crying and screaming that she wanted "Mama" (presumably Ines/Carmen)—thanks, Catherine! Thanks for your support!—and then we voted again, just to be safe, in the Community Center (without Catherine this time), and, after we'd had a few drinks, we voted for a third time, under the name "Mr. and Mrs. Iwanna Eggplant" at the local Chrysler dealership. At least I think we did; that part of the day is a little fuzzy. So we were definitely doing our part, but, unfortunately, many other supporters and probable supporters and theoretical supporters chose to be self-ish and lazy and didn't bother to vote, which severely reduced my final numbers. Andrew and I had proven that voting need not be a chore and that, in fact, it was possible to have fun while voting if you adopted the right attitude by drinking and taking drugs and having sex in the car while devoting an entire day to doing it.

Although the endorsements had not exactly poured in, I had gotten a few. However, none of these, other than Rod Longpole's, were able to boost turnout significantly, at least not in my favor. The crack-dealing crowd was behind me 100 percent, to be sure, but the ominous pools of bloody vomit that I noticed on the city's sidewalks as I went to vote brought a grim foreboding that "Big Crack" was going to let me down on Election Day. Sure enough, a bad batch of crack laden with deadly rat poison had gone around town in the last week of October, turning many Meyer supporters into drooling morons. I pride myself on my lack of prejudice, so let me be com-pletely clear here. Drooling morons' votes are *every bit* as valuable as those of the usual "garden variety" kind of morons one finds at a standard American polling place. That is our system, and I respect it. But when you're too brain-damaged or dead to actually vote, well then, I think you don't have anything to complain about when crack remains illegal and the "crackhead lifestyle" remains on the margins of American society. Given half a chance, I would have taken up both the shield of justice and the sword of righteousness on behalf of Bal-timore's oppressed crackhead minority, but since they had shown themselves unwilling to make more than a token effort on my behalf,

I resolved that I would not raise a finger to help them. It is very much beside the point that, having lost the election, I was fundamentally powerless to help or harm them. The salient issue is that, having now learned firsthand how sneaky and unreliable drug addicts can be, I became a lifelong opponent of drugs and drug abuse and have led the fight against the crackheads who f-cked me over back in 1998.

I can hear you asking whether my opponent Porter Marshall had poisoned my supporters' crack with rat poison. Certainly many people said that he had. But, to be fair, we will never know, since he died when a helicopter he had chartered to bring food and medicine to Honduras after a disastrous series of mudslides crashed into the Gulf of Mexico. This time, his predecessor's twenty-year-old wife could not be deterred from running to fill Marshall's seat and lost after it turned out that the fall campaigning season coincided with a trip to Greece that she had won at a charity auction.

The winner?

Me.

The "People's House." That's what we call the House of Representatives, maybe, and it truly is full of people. Probably around four hundred members, to be exact. Maybe even more. Can you imagine all those people in one place? I've never been a sports fan (and I don't like people who are), but once, when I was little, my dad took me to an Orioles game because a client had given him some tickets. There were a lot of people in that baseball stadium, and I didn't care for it much. In fact, I made my father leave and take me to a toy store after a few baskets had been scored. Maybe it was football. The point is I've never been terribly fond of large groups of people and, if it is one thing, Congress is full of people. Each of them terrified of getting kicked out of Washington and having to go back to Emphoria, Kansas, or whatever for the rest of their lives. So it is intense. John Quincy Adams died in the Capitol, and you can see why. It's just a lot.

So what kind of people are elected to the House of Representatives? I began to realize, after just a few weeks in Congress, that almost all of them were complete and total losers. I know, I know. They must have been "winners" in some sense in order to "win" the election in whatever godforsaken place they came from. But in pretty much every other respect they were exactly the sort of people you would have bullied in high school. The bullies go to the Senate, the saying goes; their victims go to the House.

I won't deny that it was a severe blow to learn how uncool the House of Representatives is. I had fought my way past the velvet ropes, imagining a glamorous club crowded with leggy supermodels and rich, fat Middle Eastern businessmen with fingers like sausages straining against pinky rings encrusted with sapphires and rubies (rubies, which are Mike McLintock's birthstone, have always been one of my favorite gems) who paw at them while stone-faced bodyguards keep interlopers at a respectful distance, and shirtless muscle-bound waiters serve magnums of Dom Perignon as throbbing techno music plays. *That* was what I had imagined. The reality was far, far different. The point is, don't believe everything you learn in school about how cool the House of Representatives is. It may be a lot of things, but "cool" isn't one of them.

What can I say? I was young and naive. I had hoped for glamor, style, intrigue, and even a whiff of sex. Instead I got the nerd (not that there is anything wrong with nerds! See Chapter One or Two) table. Right away, I noticed that in addition to being ugly, everyone was terribly dressed. I mean outlet center bad. The cheap suits on the men looked like they might burst into flames at any point, as the volatile Vietnamese chemicals they were made from decomposed, but compared to the women, they looked like late-'80s era Don Johnson. Oh, my God, you've never seen such women. Fat and either flat as a board or with giant opera singer bosoms—none of them were much to look at to begin with. But they did themselves no favors when they chose their garments, their lavender patent-leather kitten heels, or their shiny heavy-duty industrial-strength pantyhose. Their makeup invariably appeared to have been applied with a mason's trowel, and their lipstick was worn in a manner made popular by Bozo the Clown (see illustration).*

But it was their hairstyles that I found the most soul-destroying. I've heard that, in many small towns, the local beautician will make a little extra money on the side by preparing corpses at the town's funeral home. This is something you would certainly believe to be true after glancing around the House of Representatives for no more than just a few moments. They say that bad taste is contagious. After barely a week in the House, I began to have a recurring nightmare that dogs me to this day. In it, I am being attacked by the other female members of Congress, who hold me down and administer a ridiculous permanent wave. I wake in tears, clawing at my scalp, screaming, "Get it off! Get it off!"

Bad breath has always been a personal bugaboo of mine. Something about the decaying death smell of really bad breath makes me physically ill. And the sense memory of it will linger for hours, so that I seem to still smell it long after the offending party has departed. I guess I was prepared for a certain amount of bad breath in Congress. I had seen the House, of course, on television and may have even

---

* Illustration missing due to copyright and budget restrictions.

visited it during a Model UN trip to Washington, where I was either drunk or hungover to such an extent that I can't even remember if I visited the House of Representatives. Suspecting that, mainly because there were so many old Members, there would inevitably be some bad breath, I had steeled myself and avoided to the greatest extent possible having conversations in noisy places, which sometimes require the other person to speak at a close distance in order to be heard. As we halitosisphobes can attest, it is in these close conversations when bad breath is most likely to make itself known, sneaking up on you in circumstances that make it hard to recoil without seeming rude, even though every fiber of your being is telling you to run.

Like I say, I knew there would be some bad breath. What shocked me was the scope of the problem. While I don't personally use Scope mouthwash (I prefer the more upscale Cepacol, and if that makes me a snob, well, sue me!), I came to understand how apt the name is when I began to grasp the dimensions of the bad breath problem in the House. The scope of it was, quite literally, breathtaking.

But what could one do? One couldn't simply remain holed up in one's office, communicating with the outside world only through trusted associates with consistently fresh breath from a safe distance that made it unlikely one would even have to smell their breath in the first place. Or could one? And if one hired mostly younger staff members, regardless of experience, one might be able to avoid the unpleasant aromas that often attend dentures and other types of dental work. And younger people are often more breath-conscious generally, lacking the arrogance of older people who often seem completely indifferent to the way they smell. In terms of whether or not to hire married people, one faced a dilemma. Single people might be on the prowl for a mate and more likely to brush and floss frequently in order to be as sexually attractive as possible but, on the other hand, married people would have someone with whom they were theoretically intimate enough to warn them of offending odors. Sure, this comparatively antisocial approach to governing might limit the impact one could have, but when it came to a choice between getting your name on a lot of bills that probably were going to pass or fail regardless of your support and dealing with a lot of mouth-f-rting, well, that was a no-brainer.

Look, here's another reason why Congressmen are such losers: There's no real money in it. A member of the House of Representatives makes $174,000 a year, which may be a lot to some of these people, but to you and me it's nothing more than chump change. Of course, the real reward is having the honor to serve. But if America wanted to attract a higher class of person, who dresses more fashionably, to public service, it might consider making it pay a little better.

Let's take a look at some of the other perks. Is there free parking? I can't remember. There may well have been. But keep in mind that whatever you're getting, at least four hundred other members are also getting, so it's not like it's particularly *exclusive.* Can you get tables at new trendy restaurants? Sometimes yes, sometimes no. Can you get on a plane before everyone else? You can, but ordinary people who are waiting in line will sometimes get mad at you and then turn out to be reporters for *The Hill.* Is there a gym? Yes, but after visiting it once and having nowhere to look but at sweaty, gross Congressmen, I never went back. Sure, you get an office, which is something I had never really had before, since associates at my law firm were forced to work in an open area outside the partners' private offices. And you got a staff. It was during my first term that I made the acquaintance of such lifelong associates as Amy Brookheimer and Dan Egan, both comparatively youthful at the time and relatively odorless if not entirely sweet-smelling.

I would not want you to believe that I was a complete hermit during this first brush with elected office. There were a few other members whose company I was able to tolerate, even sometimes enjoy. These were mostly other scions of wealthy families, whose clothing budgets were not dictated by their Congressional salaries and whose taste had not been determined by what was on sale in size XXL at Target. And there were some older members who, like Abe Blumfeld had done, took me under their wing and sought to give me guidance. I recall one such mentor, then-Speaker Mario Nicastro, who had represented Boston's North End for decades, saying to me as I sat on his lap and his hands moved rapidly under my shirt attempting to undo my bra (which, ironically, had a clasp in front), "Martha [he always called me Martha], in Congress you're either a workhorse or a show horse." As someone who had been showing horses pretty much since the time she could walk, I resolved that I would be the latter.

And so I set out to make my mark, with a few showy maneuvers that would get me just enough attention to be able to claim credit for anything that was popular when it came time to run for reelection. This, it turned out, was a bit harder than it looked. When I think of the bills I introduced, H.Res.1063: "Designating room H-226 of the United States Capitol as the 'Lincoln Room,'" and H.Res.1068: "Recognizing Hispanic Heritage Month and celebrating the heritage and culture of Latinos in the United States and the immense contributions of Latinos to the United States," which I introduced with my good friend Representative Taguilas, who now looks like a fat cook in a food truck but back in those days was *muy caliente*, or H.R.6790: "To amend the Internal Revenue Code of 1986 to clarify that gain or loss on the sale or exchange of certain coins or bullion for strictly numismatic purposes be exempt from recognition," which I introduced after an informative conversation at the home of one of my constituents, I can't help but regret that none of those bills left committee.

On the other hand, we did rename a post office after one of Maryland's own daughters, Anna Ella Carroll, who had the wisdom and good grace (not to mention the foresight) to free her slaves before Emancipation, and deserves recognition for that.

Memories of the House . . . What else? I remember Representative Langon Kruger of Nebraska cornering me in the cloakroom and going on and on about why I had to vote for some place or another to become a National Grassland and thinking, "My God, this is actually important to this guy." That was eye-opening. And of course Representative Dan Chase of the West Palm Beach area, remember him? We went to Italy on a fact-finding trip together, and he introduced me to a lot of women I later learned were prostitutes. So in this way I put in my pocket the gold coin of experience—the only coin that may never be spent.

When one looks past the shabby, smelly members of Congress shuffling about in their sad, forlorn way and opens one's eyes to the splendors of the Capitol building and the District of Columbia generally, it is sometimes possible to forget the moral squalor that attends governing at the junior varsity benchwarmer level in the House. The Capitol itself is a magnificent building despite its stupid spelling. I won't deny that parts of it can be a bit tacky (but never tackier than the people inside it), and there are cynical crowd-pleasing "politically correct" recent additions of statues and paintings and plaques honoring Native Americans and women and what-have-you. That kind of thing can't be helped, and you just have to smile and grin and walk quickly whenever you see the signs that workmen are about to unveil yet another statue of a Hawaiian princess or some g-ddamn thing.

What else can I tell you about the Capitol? Well, if the brochure they give your former press secretary when he runs over to get it is to be believed, the Capitol dome is 288 feet high and 96 feet in circumference. Or maybe diameter. Which one is the "across" one? While far from the biggest dome in the world or even the country, it is plenty big enough to serve its purpose, which is somewhat unclear. Anyone who has ever lived in a house with a round room or even a semicircular portion of a room that is otherwise square knows how hard they are to put furniture in. Believe it or not, the Capitol was built during the height of the Civil War, when brother fought against brother and battles raged from the Atlantic seaboard all the way to the Western frontier, which would have been probably near or even past the Mississippi River. I defy even the most confirmed cynic to stand in the center of the Capitol and not find it inspiring when they look up and imagine the relief the workmen building it must have felt not to have been drafted as soldiers. Sure, the work was dangerous and the end result is kind of all over the place aesthetically, but at least they weren't getting their wounded limbs amputated by a drunk with a dull saw or sh-tting their dysentery-infected innards out in some prison camp.

The Capitol is made of marble, some incredible amount of it, too, like five hundred tons, which symbolizes the strength and endurance of our great nation. Like America, marble can never be broken, except by relentless hammering or with a kind of vibrating saw that goes through it like butter.

On the left side as you face the building (but on the right side if you are looking out from inside it or are outside but facing the back of the building) is the House of Representatives, the B-side to the institution, which has expanded far beyond the space originally alloted to accommodate the representatives of America's ever-growing population. Listen, I am all for immigration and for Americans having babies, but what it has done to the House chamber is a total disgrace. On the rare occasion there was a rare occasion that all the Congressmen had to attend, such as the State of the Union Address or some kind of ceremonial event, we were crammed in like sardines, and the breath problem, in particular, became extremely acute.

"A woman's place is in the House"—you've heard that, right? I even used it on my campaign poster, even though it doesn't quite work—the expression is "a woman's place is in the *home*"—but whatever, good enough for a campaign, I suppose. Not too highbrow, just very slightly witty in the way that makes dumb people feel smart when they read it. And, as any politician knows, winning elections is *all* about dumb people. But here's the thing: It turns out it's not true, because I was in the House, and I wanted to get out of there. My dissatisfaction with holding office as a Congresswoman caused a genuine personal crisis. I had reached the promised land and found it wanting. Where could I go next?

The answer was right in front of me, or rather to the right of me if I were standing in front facing the Capitol or to the left if I was looking at it from behind. That's right. You guessed it. It was the U.S. Senate.

Ask yourself, which would you rather have: a job where you have to get elected every two years, you have no power, and there's more than four hundred gross dweebs and small-town nobodies fighting for attention, or a job as a senator? Like Julius Caesar had before he became Caesar back when he was Julius Senator? I knew I had to get to the Senate, and fast.

One of the worst aspects of elective office is the "elective" part. You have to run for the godd-mn things, which means you either have to dislodge an incumbent, which is next to impossible, or find an open seat and win it, which, though slightly easier, is still extremly hard. You have to raise money; you have to hire people and recruit volunteers; you have to meet the disgusting voters and talk to some of them; and you have to get the support of the party establishment. Everybody wants something from you, whether it's influence, loyalty, or just some of your time, and believe me, if you do get elected, they will not be shy about coming to claim it. Still, I knew that the Senate was better than the House, and I didn't really feel like returning to private life just yet. I mean, sometimes I did, but I've always been moody and whimsical, and the important thing is that I know that about myself.

As luck would have it, at just about the same time as my "get me the f-ck out of here" panic attacks about being stuck in the Hellhole of Representatives were becoming unbearably acute, the senior senator from Maryland, Bobby Esposito, was shot to death by his wife after he had attempted to blame a corruption scandal involving kickbacks for federal infrastructure construction grants on her, and also f-cked her sister. That left an open seat with just a short time to go before Election Day.

I waited a decent interval to allow the party elders time to come to me and ask me to run, and when they did not, I went to them. I pride myself on a particularly acute sense of emotional intelligence, and from their restless milling around and early departure, I could tell that they were less than enthusiastic about my candidacy. I understood their hesitancy, I really did. I had been in the House for a little over three years and, because of lingering sexism, had not made much of a mark.

Nevertheless, despite not having their blessing, I went ahead and took all the steps necessary to run, eventually announcing my candidacy at the Glory Hole, a Western saloon–themed bar in Bethesda whose owner had taken a shine to me and had guaranteed me a full house by offering two-for-one backbar shots. The optics were pretty good, at least until things got utterly out of hand, and the subsequent press coverage of the wave of disorderly conduct arrests that followed kept me in the news and the public eye. At least twenty others threw their hats in the ring, which also helped, and when the dust had settled on Election Night, I had beaten the party's annointed candidate, a lifelong public servant with an extremely lackluster personality, by a handful of votes and won the election with the smallest number of votes in Senate history. Still, I was making history, and that's what is important.

The move to the Senate from the House was a comparatively simple one, akin to shifting one's locker between high school grades. But, though separated only by a long hallway with even more ugly paintings in it, the Senate was a world away from the huddled masses of the House. Cool, clean, and comparatively empty—and mostly off-limits to the press—I still recall breathing my first cleansing lungful of healthy air, untainted by the decay that lingered in the discount dental work of the denizens of the House. The senators, too, were a breed apart. They carried themselves with a certain hauteur that made an immediate impression—a very, very good impression.

As those who study these things know, the real power in the legislative branch is vested in its various committees. As a junior senator without much in the way of a popular mandate or even prior government experience, I could not be expected to have been appointed to any of the real good ones, like Finance or Intelligence, at least at first. But I also wasn't expecting what I got, which were Rules and Administration, Small Business Entrepreneurship, Indian Affairs, and Veterans' Affairs, which anyone could tell were all sh-t committees, not to mention not involving anything I knew or cared about. It looked like the empire of sexist white males had struck back at Selina Meyer, and not for the first (or last) time.

Still, it was better than being on the Select Committee on Aging, which, frankly, pretty much all the senators I saw were highly qualified for.

Yet in many respects it was déjà vu all over again. I had obtained something I thought I wanted—membership in the exclusive club of the Senate, sometimes called "the most exclusive club in the world"—and yet once I had gotten admitted, I couldn't help but think of that club in Ibiza that Andrew and I had gone to one summer during law school, where everyone was insanely attractive and raging on ecstasy, a precurser to MDMA and molly that now seems as quaint as quaaludes. Now *that* was an exclusive club, and compared to it, the Senate quickly started to seem almost as drab as the House. I attempted to put my nose to the grindstone and feign interest in the affairs of Native Americans and veterans, and looking back on it now, there were a few moments of levity and even, dare I say, fun—if no actual honeymoon—during my first few months in the Senate.

It's not widely known, but senators, perhaps by dint of their longer terms and greater job security, are incurable pranksters and cutups who never miss an opportunity to crank call each other, spend a few hours inventing some kind of fake joke bill to try and get others to sign onto, or farting loudly in the "senators only" elevator. And, of course, as has been the case for two centuries or more, the drinking and consequent drunkenness is completely out of control.

In those days, people would often say to me, "Wow! You have to be really smart to be a senator!" and I guess it's easy to see why lots of stupid people believe this. Senators often look smart, and on television, though almost never in person, they can sometimes even sound somewhat smart. But are they smart? Most of the time, no. The thing about being a senator as opposed to a mere congressman is that you get a much larger staff budget, meaning that you can hire a bunch of smart people (often for next to nothing) and get them to do the work for you and even take most of the tedious meetings with lobbyists and constituents, leaving you plenty of time to drink and play practical jokes on one another.

In addition to the larger staff and larger salary, there a few other ways that being a senator is demonstrably better than being a congressman. One of the best perks is the small hideaway office in the Capitol that each senator gets, which eliminates the need to travel on the Capitol's adorable but breakdown-prone special subway. As the name suggests, it also serves as a "hideaway" from others, and by immemorial custom, a senator is never disturbed in his or her hideaway except in the case of a vote or a bomb threat. I readily adapted to the daily routine while the Senate was in session of napping in my hideaway when not voting or being evacuated. I have always been a napper and still to this day prefer napping to most other activities, but of all the naps I have ever taken in all the many places I have been in my life, none were deeper or more restorative than those I took in the Senate in my hideaway office in the soundproof depths of the Capitol. I can feel my eyes starting to close just thinking about it.

Don't get me wrong. The last thing in the world I would want is is to seem cynical about the great work of the United States government and my own part in it. Did I attend hearings while I was in the Senate? I most certainly did. Did I sometimes ask questions during those hearings? Of course. Did I vote on things? You bet. What about bills—did I sponsor any of those? Absolutely. But when all was said and done, I just felt like the Senate was not exactly the right fit for me. The pond had gotten smaller, sure, but I was still just one of a hundred fish and by no means the biggest of those. I still enjoyed governing when I had the chance to do it, but I often felt like the other senators were in my way and preventing me from really being heard on what I thought needed to be done.

Yet again I found myself asking "Is this all there is?"

And, yet again, the answer, fortunately, was no.

CHAPTER SEVEN

A Heartbeat Away—The Vice Presidency

The telling of the full story of the Meyer vice presidency, complete with historical context, must await the future judgment of historians, in particular the sort of historians who, for some reason, study vice presidencies. I think any sane person would have to wonder what to expect from someone with such a peculiar interest and the sort of self-defeating lack of ambition that would cause them to end up spending their lives in such a dreary intellectual and academic backwater as the study of vice presidents. My greatest anxiety in this regard is that anyone who becomes a distinguished scholar of the vice presidency would be the sort of wiseass who would devote themselves to picking unusual viewpoints and uncommon pursuits as a way of annoying other people and making themselves seem more interesting than they actually are. And, as a result, that they might try to pull some bullsh-t on me. Of course, basic principles of logic dictate that one not complicate explanations beyond necessity, so it's more probable that a historian of the vice presidency is just a second-rate historian who didn't have what it takes to be a historian of the presidency.

Like many of my predecessors in the Rectangular Office, the winding path that led me there started when, having grown increasingly bored and disgusted with the Senate, I decided in the spring of 2011 after a series of conversations with close friends and advisors, to look for something better. Although I had been in the Congress a comparatively brief time, there was, nevertheless, a strong temptation to cash out by taking some sort of lobbying job and getting paid to pester my former colleagues. The problem is that—because I tend to be discriminating in my friendships and was never part of the back-slapping, bottom-pinching, hooker-punching culture that prevails in Washington's good old boys' club—I was not sure that I would have an open door when, as an outsider, I returned to lobby. Also, as an officeholder, I had become adept at avoiding lobbyists (who are almost as big a nuisance as constituents) and was worried that, once the tables were turned, I might be similarly avoided by others.

Plus, well, lobbying simply isn't "me." I've never been one to beg, to plead, to go cap in hand to others to ask for favors or special treatment. And, as is well known, lobbyists sell their services to the highest bidder just like prostitutes and, increasingly, really good electricians, at least if you want them to work on a weekend.

On the other hand, the money was good, and that was a particularly important consideration at this time in my life. I had recently become a single mom when, after twenty or so years of marriage, Andrew and I had agreed to separate, reasonably amicably. Like millions of other Americans, Andrew, he and I had learned, suffers from a disease, specifically, an addiction, more specifically, an addiction to sex, and most specifically, an addiction to sex with women who are not his wife. I am not one of those old-fashioned women who considers a husband's occasional whoopsie to be unforgivable. In fact, as a thoroughly modern woman with contemporary attitudes, I understand that men (and women!) have certain needs that they may wish to gratify outside the marital bedchamber, so to speak. A steady, stable relationship with a discreet, age-appropriate woman who was more willing to do certain kinds of things in bed and elsewhere than a wife might be even if she had once been willing to do them back in the early days of their relationship—well, I think nine out of ten wives would regard that sort of arrangement as acceptable, even desirable, as long as the woman had no designs on actually marrying the husband and having additional children with him, which might dilute the inheritance of any children from the first marriage, no matter how unworthy of inheriting anything they were.

Unfortunately, as with so many of his other business dealings, Andrew seemed unable to successfully come to an understanding with the sort of worldly and attractive-but-not-too-attractive mistress of the kind that are generally considered acceptable in this day and age. And, also as with his many businesses, he seemed unable to govern his impulses and enthusiasms and took up and discarded lovers at a dizzying pace to such an extent that these outside relationships often overlapped. Quite frequently, I would learn about them because of some kind of jealous spat between two or more of his girlfriends, which would require the intervention of the police and yet another implausible cover story as to why Andrew had a black eye or most of his hair burned off.

Like many young fathers, Andrew had an insatiable weakness for nannies and au pairs. Of course, one doesn't have to be some sort of bullsh-t psychologist or social scientist to figure out why. A young, nubile caregiver living under the same roof while the baby's mother is coping with the horror and depression that comes with giving birth is, of course, going to be sexually attractive. I never made the mistake of breast-feeding, as some women do, but, as I waited patiently and then impatiently for my milk to dry up, I will admit that the discomfort that God had decided to punish me with for having a child may have made me somewhat irritable.

And so, when Andrew proposed the notion of a live-in au pair, I was receptive, imagining a Mary Poppins type who could take the screaming baby far away to dance on a rooftop or something. Andrew being Andrew, after considerable internet research, found instead an agency that specialized in Scandinavian girls and that included a photograph and their measurements in the list of their qualifications. Liberal attitudes toward sexual matters have prevailed in those countries for centuries because, frankly, what else is there to do?

Andrew's recruiting of Scandinavian au pairs led to a half-dozen Swedish, Norwegian, Danish, and Finnish teenagers (plus one Icelandic girl, but I'm not sure if she counts) taking advantage of him. No sooner would I fire one than the agency would send another, even more attractive, to take her place. It was undoubtedly during this period when we were on the "Au Pair Train" when Andrew's sex addiction took root, and for that I will always blame myself a bit. By the time we had realized the nature of the problem and spent some time coming up with solutions, he was perhaps too far gone. An affair with Rosa, the sixty-three-year-old El Salvadoran woman we had hired to put an end to the cycle of temptation and giving into temptation that the Scandinavian girls had initiated, was the last straw. I told Andrew that he had to leave and that he could take Rosa with him, as long as she had finished the ironing. To this day, Andrew maintains that Rosa was the only woman he ever really loved. Other than me, of course.

So, there I was, bored out of my skull in the stupid Senate, feeling that special kind of disappointment you have when you expect something to be great and everything you've always wanted and it turns out instead to be Suck City. And yet lobbying seemed equally if not more disgusting. What about teaching? Don't make me laugh. And yet, I did need to earn some sort of a living because my mother, a notorious cheapskate, had declined to provide me with any sort of support in the form of even a modest trust or allowance. Faced with this sh-t smorgasbord of unpleasant options, I chose the least unappealing one: running for president.

On the one hand, of course, being elected president is every schoolboy's and many schoolgirls' dream. You get to live in the White House and fly on Air Force One and everyone has to be polite to you, blah, blah, blah. But on the other hand, you can't just become president by wishing for it; you have to *campaign* for the godd-mn office. And that means getting out and meeting (bad), listening to (worse), and touching (worst of all) lots and lots of ordinary Americans. The formal structure of campaigning requires you to stand up and ask people for something—their vote—which they consider valuable but which you, in thinking about the millions of votes it takes to be elected, regard as almost totally worthless. In exchange for this thing they consider important and you consider pathetically insignificant (I'm just being honest here), they expect you to take a sincere interest in their problems. Actually, I'm going to go out on a limb here and say that I don't even think they care much more about what you think of them than you care what they think of you. They just want someone—anyone—to listen to them hold forth on some pet peeve or theory, and since their grandkids have long ago stopped taking their calls (one thing you learn very quickly when you run for elective office is that all likely voters, regardless of politics or party, are old), they swarm like fire ants to attack the only available target and one that, because of our flawed system, is exceptionally vulnerable to their form of self-centered malice: politicians running for office.

Having run for office before, I embarked upon my presidential campaign with my eyes wide open as far as having to deal with gross, unpleasant voters went. And I had confronted the brutal calculus that every presidential candidate faces, which is that, having developed various coping mechanisms for dealing with the electorate in one's own district or state, as a presidential candidate one must make a personal face-to-face appeal to mouth-breathers in all forty-eight real states,* or at least a significant subset of them.

So why bother, you may well wonder. Why spend any time on so-called (and extremely appropriately named) retail politics if every single one of the people you try and humor is going to just spew stupid nonsense about their own problems and do so with my least favorite aromatic accompaniment: bad breath?†

The reason candidates put themselves through the ordeal of interacting with voters is quite simple, and in this case, at least initially, it played very much to my advantage. I'm speaking, of course, of the media.

I have nothing but the utmost respect for the fourth estate. I firmly believe that a free press is essential to good government and, indeed, to a properly functioning democracy. This is not to say that I have always felt fairly treated by the media. But I have also always tried to look at the matter of press coverage from the press' point of view. It must be an abject misery to have to come up with something

---

* As brutal as our current system is, no one takes Hawaii or Alaska seriously, although that day may one day come and, if it does, God help the presidential contenders then.

† To return to the topic of bad breath for just a sec, I want to explain for the benefit of posterity that the reason so many politicians appear to grimace in photographs when they are listening to the opinions of voters is that, because the environment of rallies and rope lines is often a noisy one, you have to draw very close to another person to hear what they have to say. And very often that person will have bad breath, either because they are old or because they live in some semi-civilized part of the country that, thanks to our syphilitic forefathers, has more votes in the electoral college than they remotely deserve, or just because they're the type of weirdo who would show up at a political rally in the first place.

new to write every day about a situation that mostly stays the same. I mean, can you imagine how boring it would be to be a reporter or journalist and try to arrange the same two dozen words into different stories day after day, week after week? This is why I think the best people don't go into journalism and why, if they do, they don't go into political journalism but become, instead, movie critics, which enables them to watch a lot of movies for free or, at least, to expense them.

In this case, though, the political press—prematurely exhausted by yet another primary season of dishwater-dull white men scrambling over one another in an unseemly fashion to try and distance themselves from Washington and run, during the primary, as outside-the-Beltway mavericks—turned to me as a welcome breath of fresh air or, at the very least, as something new to write about.

As it happened, I had declared my candidacy without really intending to. The preponderance, yet again, of white male candidates had inspired *The Hill*, one of Washington's confusingly unprofitable news outlets, to come up with a list of "outside the box" candidates for the presidency consisting almost entirely of women and minorities and a few people who I guess were gay and maybe not terribly happy about being singled out for being gay in this particular way. To a man—and woman and whatever—they all declared in the mini interview that accompanied their listing in the article that they did not intend to run for president—at least, not in the near future. Ha ha, wink emoji. This is, I guess, what you are supposed to do if you actually *do* intend to run for president someday in the future but are trying to dog-whistle everyone about what a smart and shrewd politician you are while also appearing to be modest and devoted to doing whatever job you have at present with utmost dedication.

And that may be all well and good for that type of conventional schemer. In my case, the reporter from *The Hill* had reached me at a bad time on a bad day when I was having trouble reaching the physician who had prescribed my antianxiety medication for a refill and when I had had to bring Catherine to the office and delegate some staff members to take care of her. As I recall, she was missing Rosa and making a god-awful racket when, having dodged the reporter for a week, I accidentally took the call, thinking it was my doctor who had a similar name. In answer to what was probably a playful question about whether I would ever want to be president, I responded somewhat testily, but also, I thought, in the playful spirit of the question, that anything would be better than being a senator where you didn't even have your own doctor or your own butler or your own airplane, for God's sake. The article ran the next day as "Senator's White House Run," and considering how dumb the whole Senate thing had turned out to be, it seemed pointless to deny it.

As luck would have it, the Senate was in the midst of one of its periodic procedural crises over the rules governing the filibuster, which, between us, I'd always considered just a chance for senators to sniff each other's f-rts while patting each other on the back for their bipartisan restraint. There's a lot of stupid sh-t like that in the Senate that's supposed to make it more gentlemanly and statesmanlike than that greased pig rodeo next door in the House, but all those stupid customs always seemed to me like just a chance for senators to relax by exercising an opportunity to show that they didn't believe in anything in particular.

Anyway, whether or not some bill or appointment or other would be filibustered and whether the opposing party would respect the filibuster was the topic du jour, though looking back on it now, I can't recall even the slightest detail. That's going to be something for those vice scholars of the vice presidency to figure out. My comments in *The Hill* about how lame the Senate was were seen not as reflecting my frustration with a lack of medication or childcare but rather with the partisan gridlock that, yet again, had ground the nation's business to a standstill. Media outlets on the left and right took up my banner as the woman willing to shake things up in Washington. My poll numbers soared, and the establishment front-runners began to look over their shoulders at the fast-approaching political dynamo from right out of nowhere.

Me.

I'd be lying if I said it wasn't fun to go from sitting in (or, more often, skipping) hearings on the seemingly intractable and endless problems of Native Americans and veterans to suddenly being skyrocketed to Washington's A++ list. The press sorted through my few public statements on the issues and, since I had made so few public statements, generally liked what they saw. What I will now admit was my genuine ignorance or naivete in my questioning of witnesses at Senate hearings was treated as a sort of brilliant Columbo-like fake ignorance or fake naivete. Some of my catchphrases, like "Maybe you covered this earlier" or "Remind me again who you are" were enshrined in some of the first internet memes as statements by cats, honey badgers, and, for some reason, a still picture of JonBenét Ramsey. Among the headlines of the time were "Might It Be 'President Meyer'?" and "Is This Meyer's Moment?" (that was a cover of *Time*, a newsmagazine, which is a type of news thing of the period—a very big deal, I can assure you).

Still, even to me, it seemed a little fast and, well, *soon*. For one thing, I simply didn't have the seasoned, well-qualified staff a viable candidate needs, having hired mostly donors' kids to work in my Senate office. And the whole "woman who speaks her mind" thing would only get me so far when someone asked me a detailed question about, you know, foreign affairs or, well, domestic affairs. To assist me, I hired Amy Brookheimer, a young woman of a type particular to federal politics who has subjugated her entire ego to that of a politician with the rationale that somehow her sacrifice serves a higher purpose either in terms of her ultimate career goals or the nation as a whole. What women like this (and they are mostly women) don't realize is that some people just aren't, if you will, officer material, and a readiness to abase yourself as a slave to another person is certain proof that you're never going anywhere except to becoming a different kind of slave. (Amy, if you are reading this, I'm sorry if it offends you, but you need to hear it from someone, even if it's by reading a book rather than in person.) Amy was by no means the best nor most qualified of this type of Beltway Bachelorette, but she was available and a little above mediocre.

And then, just as quickly as it had started, the whole "Selina Surge" was over. Because I had given them little to work with, the gnatlike attention of the media returned to the horse race among the front-runners and without any ability to raise funds to run ads in primary states, my numbers sank below the margin of error.

But still I didn't give up.

In the course of my rapid rise to national prominence, I had learned something about myself: I preferred the larger stage. In fact, I felt as though I were made for it. So, having appeared on *Meet the Press* and *Face the Nation* when my star was at its zenith, I now said yes to any TV or radio show that would provide me with some free media. Along the way, I also picked up some basic skills for dealing with the press that I probably should have learned a long time ago.

Former president and current Supreme Court justice Stuart Hughes is, as everyone knows, an affable ward heeler of the old school who came up through the ranks of the Chicago party machine. As governor of Michigan, he had forged bonds with key constituencies: public and private sector unions, manufacturers and large service sector employers, activist and civil rights groups, the civically engaged elite, the bottle-of-scotch-in-the-bottom-file-cabinet-drawer print media, and, of course, the party rank-and-file, thanks to his Rotarian good nature in public and vicious back-stabbing in private. Despite this, his reputation as a "good guy" and "someone you'd want to have a beer with" or "someone you'd want to have help you bury a body" had survived unblemished. With solid support from the donor class, Hughes emerged as the front-runner at a perfectly timed moment and seemed destined to sail to the White House even if he had picked Jeffrey Dahmer as his running mate.

If Stuart Hughes had any sort of an Achilles' heel, it was his wife, Edna, called "Eddie" for short. When Hughes was a mere governor, it was easy enough for him to keep Eddie under wraps up in her room in the governor's mansion watching *Law & Order* reruns and sobering up once a year in springtime to cut the ribbon for the annual Governor's Easter Egg Hunt. But once Hughes became a candidate for president, there was the usual clamor to know more about his wife and for him to show her off more in public. The more that his staff stressed that she was an "extremely private person," the louder the gossip grew that she was a complete nutcase or dead.

Her few attempts at public appearances ended abruptly with him hustling her offstage or pushing her away from a microphone and, like clockwork, the articles began to emerge wondering if Hughes's treatment of his wife indicated that he had a "woman problem" and, despite his fine words, whether he wasn't just another instrument or even exponent of the patriarchy.

And so Hughes came to me, or to be completely accurate, I came to him, because the meeting was in a nondescript hotel room in Lansing, Michigan, a city that has nothing but nondescript hotels. Still, I feel like he really came to me.

He began by letting me know that he was considering a number of possible running mates and thought that he should meet with me, purely as a courtesy. He asked me where I stood on various issues and seemed very favorably impressed when it quickly became clear that I had few, if any, opinions about anything or, if I did, I wasn't going to waste time explaining them to a fathead like Stuart Hughes. What the h-ll? At this point, I had little to lose, and I had already seen the value, even if it was just temporary, of standing out from the crowd in order to capture the media's attention. I made it clear to Hughes that I wasn't interested in anything less than a virtual co-presidency, with my full participation in every aspect of the president's ordinary and extraordinary work.

At the end of our meeting, Hughes told me that, thanks to my plain-speaking, I was now number three on his list of potential running mates. I told him that he could suck my cl-t and that I wasn't interested in posing next to a fossil for the next five months, even if it did make me look young. He seemed to like that, as well, and five months later I found myself standing on the stage at the Milwaukee Convention Center holding hands aloft with Stuart Hughes as his anointed running mate. Life is funny.

Sure, running for *vice* president seemed like a little bit of an anticlimax, but having come in fairly short order from the Senate and, before that, the House, it did seem as though I had been catapulted to the big leagues, with Secret Service protection, gaggles of reporters, and a specially designated bathroom wherever I went. Yet along with all the pomp went surprisingly little circumstance. As is the case for the actual vice president, there really is very little for a candidate for vice president to do other than show up at campaign events and press some disgusting flesh. The beauty part was that the Hughes team quickly decided that I had a special affinity, given my upbringing, for large net worth donors, so elegant and exclusive events in private homes or country clubs quickly replaced visits to diners, factory floors, and union halls. The sole vice presidential debate between me and my opponent, Colonel Abraham Buttrick, consisted mostly of his extended recounting of his time as a POW in Vietnam and the terrible things that were done to him during it, which I was too respectful of the sacrifices of our brave men and women in uniform to interrupt but which didn't seem to help his side much.

Hughes and I won, of course. On Election Night, I reminded Hughes of his pledge that I would have an open line to him, that I would be a key player in all important decisions, and that we would, for all intents and purposes, be co-presidents.

I never saw him again.

CHAPTER EIGHT

Second in Command

Of course, that's an exaggeration. But not much of one.

I did see President Hughes at our inauguration. We went through the standard routine, taking the oaths of office and then standing in the cold while a seemingly endless parade of military nonsense goes past. Inaugurations are pretty much all the same: a black woman sings a hymn, a choir from the president's home state performs a patriotic song, and if you're lucky no one recites a poem. As the first woman vice president, I also achieved another equally remarked-upon "first" when I attended my inauguration as a single woman, despite Andrew having made an enthusiastic attempt to reconcile so that he could attend and, in his words, "make some excellent connections." Having been to the inauguration, I can say that had he attended, he probably would have been sorely disappointed by the quality of the networking. Most of the invited guests were just dull government people and foreign dignitaries and, as for the members of the general public who were there, I ask you, who in their right mind would attend a presidential inauguration if they didn't absolutely have to?

I took the oath of office on our family Bible, which had been hastily purchased for the occasion at a Georgetown used bookstore. If I had still had a husband, I supposed he would have held the Bible but, since I didn't, I had asked my daughter, Catherine, then nineteen years old, to do it, and as usual, she let me down. My longtime assistant, Gary Walsh, had purchased a tasteful and flattering pale rose wool Oscar de la Renta dress with a matching coat and hat for her to wear. But Catherine being Catherine, she threw a fit and declared that the dress "wasn't her" and that she "hated it." I made it clear that she had no choice in the matter, but somehow she managed to change into a flowery, hippie-ish Betsey Johnson dress that was not only entirely inappropriate for such a dignified occasion but also much too light for the blustery, twenty-eight-degree weather. Catherine's uncontrollable shivering caused the Bible to shake so much that I barely managed to get through the oath without her dropping it. Way to go, Catherine!

After I told Catherine to go and wait in the car, I posed for the obligatory official photos with Hughes and Edna, his heavily medicated wife. And here I learned an interesting thing. You've probably observed, like I have, that people on these formal occasions often have a bit of small talk that appears to amuse all parties when they greet each other. One person says something to the other and then everyone smiles and laughs. And that's exactly what happened with Hughes and me at our inauguration. Hughes approached, smiled, and asked me "what's the best part about sex with twenty-eight-year-olds?" When I looked a bit confused, he continued, "There are twenty of them!" In the nine or ten other times we met during the three years I served as his vice president, he repeated this joke every time. I never learned whether it was something special he did just for me or whether that was his opener with everyone. I was present when Hughes welcomed the pope to America. Hughes, a Catholic, kissed his ring and then said something to him that no one else could hear and they both smiled and laughed. I have no way of knowing if it was the joke about sex with eight-year-olds, but the pope always seemed like an incorrigible pederast, so I'd bet good money that it was.

As every school child—or at least every schoolchild who is not at a sh-tty inner city public school—knows, one of the vice president's weighty responsibilities is to preside as the president of the Senate, which means that every so often you get to break a tie (woo-hoo!) but also that once a year, you welcome the actual president to the Senate to deliver the State of the Union address. So I would see Hughes then (and learn anew what was so great about sex with twenty eight-year-olds) and now and again at something like a pope-welcoming. But otherwise, the partnership I had been promised never materialized. Yet again, I was being reminded that everyone had it out for Selina Meyer, and if she was going to accomplish anything, she was going to have to do it entirely on her own.

John Nance Garner, who was vice president at some point, famously described the job as "not worth a pitcher of warm p-ss." In my stock speech as vice president, I would open with this quote and then quip, "Well, at least it was warm!" That always got a laugh or a chuckle or a favorably disposed silence, even though, between us, I have no idea what I was talking about. There's no reason that warm p-ss would be that much worse than cold p-ss, and it would probably be considerably better than scalding hot p-ss.

I resolved on my first day in my office in the Eisenhower Executive Office Building, a drafty Victorian pile next door to the White House, fittingly named after our dullest president, that I would try my darndest to make the vice presidency worth more than a warm pitcher of p-ss. Much more! I was young, I was shapely, and I was determined. After reviewing the many areas of interest that had occupied my time in the House and Senate, I decided that my first big signature effort would be to start a Clean Jobs Initiative, a partnership between business, labor, academia, and government to encourage the creation of well-paying jobs in the alternative energy sector and other environmentally forward-looking businesses. To kick it off, I decided to recruit a task force of leaders in all these fields who could identify some marquee projects that were shovel-ready so that we could make a splash quickly and get the attention of the media and generate excitement among the general public.

And here I had my first experience of running into the brick wall that President Hughes and his advisors had seemingly built around me. Somehow, every move I made, every plan I wanted to announce, every person I wanted to consult bumped up against something they were doing already but hadn't had the courtesy to tell me about. I can't say for certain that his team was doing it deliberately, although they were. After six or seven thwarted efforts, I figured out what was going on. Underneath his avuncular, hail-fellow-well-met exterior, Hughes, like so many politicians, was vain, petty, and vindictive. He just couldn't bear the idea that I would steal a tiny corner of the limelight from him for even a second. When he allowed me to do anything at all, it was only to gather up the most humiliating and trivial crumbs from under his table. The events he sent me to as his surrogate were always so stupid that, by sending me, he seemed to be making a statement about how unimportant they were. It can be difficult to be placed in social or diplomatic situations in which your very presence is intended as a calculated insult. That's how I saw it, and I'm sure that many of the audiences I appeared before felt the same way. Some clearly didn't, but the level of enthusiasm shown by D-listers was its own sort of insult, in this case to me. "What kind of weirdo would want to be liked by *these* people?" I often asked myself.

As a senator, I had had some experience with the filibuster, an arcane procedure by which a few senators could use Senate rules and customs to thwart the will of the majority. It seemed pretty crazy to me—or, at least, very confusing—and I never quite got the hang of it. As president of the Senate, as well as a former senator, reforming the Senate's procedures seemed like a natural sphere of activity for me. A few months into my first year, I had a bill drafted for filibuster reform that quickly gathered a large number of sponsors. It was a terrible disappointment to me when it was voted down almost unanimously with all of its sponsors voting against it, something that had never happened before. I had hoped, at least, that if it wasn't going to pass, at least it would be because it was filibustered, but sadly that didn't prove necessary.

There were some fleeting glimmers of success. A task force on obesity, to which President Hughes was kind enough to appoint me as chair, issued a report and some guidelines that were featured on one of the morning news shows—the second most popular one, if memory serves. The task force's recommendations included the utilization of a furry mascot called "Cookie Monster" who encouraged kids to make comically poor food choices. It turned out that a very similar character had been copyrighted by some rapacious show business people who, seeing an opportunity for some free publicity for their own character, served us with a cease-and-desist order. But I wasn't so easily defeated. Cookie Monster was to see life a few years later when, renamed Derwerd the Fur Nerd, he would testify before Congress on a different but related topic.

As people like to say about the weather, the post office is broken but nobody seems to know how to fix it. I am very proud that, despite an almost total lack of support from the president, as the head of the Postal Reform Commission, I was able to reduce the operating deficit of the U.S. Post Office from $65 billion to just over $62 billion.

Nevertheless, as someone who prides herself on honest self-assessment, I can say that my notable successes as vice president were not as many as I might have liked, though still more than other vice presidents, I'm sure.

But as I was struggling to try to do what I always try to do—change ordinary people's lives for the better through wise and compassionate government—Stuart Hughes was having troubles of his own.

A devastating series of losses in the 2014 midterm elections caused our party to lose its majority in the House, which put most of Hughes's legislative agenda into deep freeze. Ha ha. Now he would see how it felt.

More devastating still was the Uzbek hostage crisis, which began later that year. When it became clear that Hughes had known all along that one of the hostages was actually an American spy and that he had overridden my plan to avoid a government shutdown in order to distract the public's attention from the crisis, his favorability rating cratered. His support from the senior leadership in the party evaporated, and his opponents began whispering about possible impeachment.

As these various dramas played out in the public arena, behind the scenes, Edna Hughes, who had never been on a terribly solid psychological footing, had taken a turn for the worse. White House gossip had it that, since her appearance at the inauguration, she had rarely left her room, preferring to stay in bed watching an endless cycle of *Law & Order* reruns. Since new *Law & Order*s are always being made and so many had already been made, Abigail believed that she would never run out of new ones and this, it was said, was a source of great comfort to her. For his part, Hughes concocted some sort of cover story about her having an inflamed cyst in some sort of private area, which the press, in its wisdom, chose not to probe further.

What Hughes didn't count on was the fact that, if you watch them for fifteen hours a day, even *Law & Order* reruns eventually run out. Around Christmas of that year, for the first time Edna saw an episode of *Law & Order* she had seen already, and it drove her 'round the bend. She attempted suicide by drinking a yogurt beverage belonging to one of the White House maids that she had found in a cleaning closet and mistakenly believed to be drain cleaner. She was rushed to the hospital, had her stomach pumped, and survived no more the worse for wear than before, which was pretty bad to begin with. It was the last straw for the beleaguered president. On January 24, 2016, President Stuart Hughes resigned, making Selina Catherine Meyer the forty-fifth president of the United States.

That's right. Me.

CHAPTER NINE

The Meyer Era Is Inaugurated— A Blind Date with History

"So, what's it like to be president?" That's what people often ask me when I get stuck next to them in a stalled receiving line. Such a dumb question. I have experimented with various answers over the years and have yet to find one that is perfect for every occasion. For a while I tried, "It's like being an elevator operator. It has its ups and downs." But the sad, century-long decline in manned elevators made this riposte more confusing than witty. The "ups and downs" thing, of course, works with other premises, e.g., "it's like riding a donkey's d-ck" or "it's like riding an orangutan's d-ck," but most of them are not all-purpose, being inappropriate for, for example, church groups or a PTA.

When my longtime associate Kent Davison brought me the news that President Hughes was resigning to tend to his ailing wife, I was at a union hall in New Hampshire doing some early campaigning for the 2016 presidential race. Although I had always believed it was my destiny to be president, I was, nevertheless, stunned by the news. The fact that I was campaigning to be president *in the future* and yet had become president *in the present* made the whole even more mind-boggling and confounding. There are a bunch of good sayings about answered prayers, and here I was, my prayers having been answered, ready to prove the validity of some or all of them.

As a candidate, I had begun to outline what I would do if I were elected president, emphasizing many of the priorities that have been front and center throughout my political career: clean jobs, healthy eating choices for children, others. I would now have a window of opportunity, albeit not a very long one, to push my agenda forward. Not only that, I would be much better situated for my presidential campaign as the incumbent president than in the always faintly ridiculous role of vice president. In short, I was jubilant. Becoming president of the United States was unquestionably a career high for me. The satisfaction in having proved the haters and the naysayers wrong, in having the last laugh over those who had called me "superficial" and "incompetent" and "too beautiful to be president," was, well, hugely satisfying.

"Blah-blah-blah, get to the good stuff," right?

Is Air Force One cool? Oh my God, yes. Later on, when the charm of being president had somewhat worn off, I never ceased to enjoy flying around in my own giant airplane with a queen(!)-size bed and a real shower, not just one of those hand-washer things like they have on bigger yachts. If you suffer from jet lag, as I do, as well as that sort of gritty, dirty feeling you get after longer flights, well, let me tell you that having Air Force One at your disposal takes care of both of those problems right quick. Plus, no more airport security lines, no more customs, no more flight delays. In fact, the Secret Service will actually delay *other* flights in order to make sure that the president takes off in time.

How is the food on Air Force One? It's great! It's not just, you know, Air Force food, it's actually prepared by a real chef who will make whatever the president wants. And it's served on real china, even if that adds some weight and requires a little more fuel to fly around than paper or plastic. Come on, man! This is Air Force One! The first time I flew on Air Force One, they offered me a choice of possible meals and snacks but, after a while, they began to know my preferences and would just have the necessary ingredients on board. That's the kind of service you get on Air Force One. Is 24/7 access to Air Force One the best part about being president? Unquestionably yes. Any president who tells you otherwise is straight-up lying. In fact, for presidents of the Air Force One era, I think it's safe to say that, though they may run for president for other reasons, if they run for reelection four years later, Air Force One has a lot to do with it.

Maybe you've flown on a private plane once or twice in your life. I'm not talking about someone's dinky Cessna or Beechcraft. Everyone's done that. I mean a bigger plane with a bathroom. And maybe you think that's what flying on Air Force One is like. Well, it's not. Or maybe you think it's like a better kind of private aircraft that movie stars or billionaires use. Well, guess what? It's even better than that. Look, this conversation isn't really going anywhere. You just don't seem to get it. Air Force One is much better than any plane that anyone else has anywhere. You can start a nuclear war from Air Force One. That's how great it is.

Okay, what's the White House like? It's a dump! In its defense, it was built a long time ago—more than a hundred years ago—when I suppose standards were different. We all know that great story about President Taft and the bathtub. But while standards of luxury, as well as standards of living generally, may have improved very considerably since the White House was built and considered "luxurious," the people "in charge" of the White House, whoever they may be, seem to have made little effort to keep pace. The best you can say about it is that it looks sort of like someone's grandma's house, which is pleasant enough if you like your grandma, which I didn't particularly. To give you some idea, the White House is not remotely comparable to a Four Seasons in a big city like New York or Chicago or a foreign capital. Recently, though, I've noticed that the Four Seasons people have become very promiscuous in their relationships and have opened hotels in lots of second- and third-tier cities, like St. Louis and Houston. That's sort of what the White House is like. Like a franchised Four Seasons hotel in an American city with a population of less than two million people.

The Four Seasons, though, has famously comfortable beds due to, I'm told, a particular brand of mattress they use. The White House beds are nowhere near as comfortable, or at least they weren't as comfortable until I told the stewards to get some good mattresses like they have at the Four Seasons.

The mattress situation is emblematic of my early days in the White House. Even some of the simplest things I wished to have done proved difficult, with the stuffy establishment proving stubbornly resistant to my earnest efforts to make revolutionary change in the "business-as-usual" climate that prevails inside the Beltway.

Okay. But we're getting off track. What about the other perks? The president's helicopter, Marine One, is terrific. It's no insult to the Marines to say that it's good but not as great as Air Force One. It's a helicopter—what do you expect? It does have a proper toilet. And lots of the other stuff is very nice. When you're in the White House, you can ask for food at any time of the day or night. And if you're bored or restless, there are always people there to talk to. The Situation Room, for example, is manned at all hours by liaison staff from the Department of Defense. The downside is that most of these people are *extreeeeeeeemely* dweeby kids in their late twenties and early thirties in the kind of cheap J. Crew and Banana Republic officewear that just makes you want to kill yourself. So they are not exactly a lot of fun to talk to unless you're interested in, you know, global flashpoints and that kind of thing.

Can you call anyone, anywhere? Yes! Almost everyone is happy to get a call from the president of the United States, unless, of course, you're calling them to say how sorry you are that their son or daughter was killed in some kind of military silliness somewhere. And, honestly, that kind of call is one that you have to make more often than the fun kind when you call the queen for her birthday or that kind of thing.

What about the hotline to Moscow? No. That's long gone. I'm told they took it out after Nixon kept drunk-dialing Brezhnev in the middle of the night. And the "football"? The nuclear launch codes? The "button" upon which the president has his or her finger? That, actually, is all real.

Perhaps no symbol of presidential power is as potent as the nuclear "football" that enables him (or her!) to start a nuclear war at any time of the day or night. It's called the football, but it's actually a briefcase, a bit larger than normal, carried by a uniformed military aide (way to be subtle, military!). But what exactly is in the briefcase? Well, I probably shouldn't be telling you this, but it's mostly a bunch of cheap-looking loose-leaf notebooks along with a very goofy-looking EMP-hardened cell phone that supposedly enables the aide to communicate with the Pentagon or NORAD in a time of crisis, but honestly, I wouldn't count on it. The basic idea is that, if the president feels like starting a nuclear war, he or she calls over the aide and asks them to get a general or admiral on the phone and then reads them a code from one of the notebooks and then *boom!*

I won't deny that the power to annihilate the earth's entire population and turn the planet into a lifeless, radioactive wasteland for millions of years has a tendency to go to one's head. By the way, that business about cockroaches being the only creatures that would survive a nuclear holocaust? I can put that canard to rest right now. Although it may have been true when I took office, I had the bomb yields adjusted so that cockroaches would all be killed as well. I can't stand cockroaches or, as we used to call them in Palm Beach (my mother, who died while I was running for president, by the way, had a great house on the Intercoastal in Palm Beach or, technically, Gulfstream), palmetto bugs.

Along with the excitement about what I *could* do came the unpleasant realization that, other than kill everyone or swap out the White House mattresses (as well as the one on Air Force One—I said that it had an actual bedroom, right?), there was surprisingly little that I could accomplish on my own initiative. I had spent three years in the vice president's office imagining that I was being excluded from momentous decision-making, but I had failed to learn a rather obvious lesson that was staring me in the face the whole time. Hughes had proved unable to accomplish pretty much anything significant in office. All those meetings that he had kept me out of had amounted to nothing more than a lot of empty d-ck-measuring sessions.

As presidents have learned over and over, being president is not the same as being king or emperor. That's our system, and I suppose we have to accept it. In order to get anything done, you need the cooperation of the House and Senate and, in many cases, the courts, which seem to be able to make a nuisance of themselves almost constantly. And if the media take a particular like or dislike to something you're trying to do, well, those jackals are perfectly capable of torpedoing it just to satisfy their own limp egos.

At least now I would be in the meetings and I would be setting the agenda. Maybe I wouldn't accomplish everything I attempted, but I would at least be making the attempt. That said, there are a million different things a president can get behind; she can commit the government to vast new enterprises like rebuilding infrastructure or putting a man (or woman!) on Mars, or she can seek to rein in the size and reach of government by slashing regulations and cutting taxes. And then once you've decided if you're a "big government type" or a "small government type" (and, confusingly, regardless of which one you are, you have to tell everyone that you're a small government type), you have to get specific and start choosing between, say, school lunch programs or giant mass transit projects or billion-dollar weapons systems. It gets exhausting very quickly. Or—and I don't know why I'm telling you this because the odds of someone reading this book becoming president are incredibly small—you can kind of wait and see what happens, like a financial crisis or a war, and then just kind of try and deal with it as best you can. That way you're less likely to get blamed for things. I mean, you can always be blamed for *mishandling* some situation, sure, but that's usually a less bad kind of blame than you get for having *caused* it.

Another thing you can do is wait and see what sort of ideas Congress generates, since those lazy clowns are supposed to be the ones who originate legislation in the first place. And, believe me, every single one of them has a trillion ideas for how to spend the taxpayer's money, almost always on make-work boondoggles for their own districts. You can't blame them, really. People like their politicians to bring home the bacon, and politicians, especially congressmen who have to campaign all the godd-mn time, like to have a big slab of bacon like a job-retraining center or, better yet, a sports stadium to campaign in front of.

But if you just represent some district with a hundred thousand people in it, it's pretty easy to figure out what's going to keep them happy and make them like you. It's so much harder when you're president and have to try and please everyone all the time, including millions of people who don't agree on anything. But the important thing is not to lose sight of the fundamental things that you yourself believe in because, in the end, that's something you can always rely on when your advisors, the polls, and the press let you down.

So, that's the important thing. Believing in something and knowing what that is.

Okay, so getting back to the questions people always ask about being president. Is it true that the White House has a swimming pool and a bowling alley? Yes. Yes, it has both. In fact, it has two pools, an indoor one and an outdoor one. The thing is: I'm not really a swimmer or a bowler, so neither the pools nor the bowling alley were of much use to me. And even if I were a swimmer, I don't think I'd really enjoy using the pool. You see, the indoor pool was a favorite trysting spot for JFK, and even after all these years I think it would be hard for me to escape the sensation that some of his sperm was still alive and swimming around in the pool with me or, even worse, trying to crawl up inside me. Maybe it would be just one or two of them but if anyone's sperm could survive fifty years in a chlorinated pool, it was JFK's.

CHAPTER TEN

Crisis to Crisis—
The Testing of a President

On the campaign trail, one of my most popular applause lines was a pledge to be "a proactive president rather than a reactive president." Of course, reading that now, it seems like a pretty lame thing to say. But the word "proactive" was popular then or, rather, it had been popular elsewhere about five years prior, which meant that politicians were just beginning to use it, about three years after most other people had stopped. What does "proactive" mean, exactly? Well, I think it probably means something like "active," but no one is really sure. In any case, that's what it meant when I said it; that I would be an *active* president, that I would *do* things rather than just have things done *for* me or done *to* me. And that's something I actually intended to do even if the person writing my speeches expressed it in an unnecessarily roundabout way by using a made-up word.

I haven't always been well-served by the people under me—the case of the dumb speech and meaningless promise alluded to above being a great example. In fact, when cleaning up one of their messes or coping with their latest display of stunning incompetence, I've often wondered why the people who go to work in government or for politicians are so uniformly feebleminded. My best guess is that public service seems like a refuge from the real world for people who either are too lazy for the real world or know themselves well enough to understand that they couldn't really handle it, sort of in the same way that teaching is. Time and time again I would fire some weak sister (or brother!) on my team only to discover in very short order that their replacement was even worse. If one wants to avoid a slow, steady decline in overall quality, one has to then go back and find the person you just fired, fire the new person you hired to replace him (or her!), and then hire the old person back, sometimes at a higher salary. Thus, *bad* people are constantly getting raises just because they're not the *worst possible* people. This incentivization of mediocrity is a big problem in Washington, although people don't like to talk about it. My view is that you paid good money for this book, and you deserve to know.

This persistent problem of staff mediocrity would not be as severe a problem if one worked, say, in some kind of fast-food business or dentistry, but when it comes to the presidency, we're talking about decisions that are literally matters of life and death, so you really would prefer to have competent people handling them.

In some cases, as when you send our fantastic military forces into a situation in which some of them will probably die, the "life or death" aspect of the decision is obvious, especially to the men (and women!) who get killed and their families. But in other cases, like complicated choices involving health care or tax policy, the consequences may not seem so dire at first, but you can wind up killing millions in the long run if you're not careful. Let's say you decide to take some money away from disease research in order to help fund, oh, I don't know, something involving making the Panama Canal wider. And then, fifteen years later, some kind of previously unknown disease starts killing people in Africa (which is where these kinds of things seem to always happen) and, before long, it has spread to the rest of the world, perhaps through the now slightly wider Panama Canal. Now, if you hadn't cut funding for disease research, maybe you could have stopped it. But here's the thing: The connection is always going to be a bit tenuous, and because it took so long for the problem to develop, you're probably out of office and, even if someone did find a way to blame you, it wouldn't do much damage. Whereas if you go ahead with the Panama Canal thing, you get to cut a ribbon and get a lot of donations from shipping companies, both of which will benefit you when it really matters, in the here and now rather than in the if and when.

My publisher has suggested that providing a revealing window on presidential decision-making would really set this book apart from other presidential memoirs, in which former presidents tend to mince words in order to paint themselves in a flattering light. No president ever writes a book called *Boy, I Sure F-cked Up*, though if they did I bet it would sell a lot more than one called *My Story* or *My Journey* or some other very "first thought" kind of idea.

Presidential decision-making works much like other sorts of decision-making, except that instead of "Should I go to the store?" you're asking yourself, "Should I bomb Yemen?" But to stick with the comparison for a moment, much of your initial calculation is likely to be the same. You'll ask yourself, "Can I do it?" "Should I do it?" "Can I afford it?" "Will it accomplish what I want?" etc. In the case of going to the store, those questions are usually fairly easy to answer. As a prominent public official for several decades, I'm not really much of a store-goer, but back when I used to go, before I had someone to go for me, I always used to find myself putting all kinds of extra things into my shopping cart that weren't on my shopping list. These impulses can be very hard to control when shopping—or when bombing Yemen.

The process of presidential decision-making should always include input from knowledgeable experts. Listen to the experts! Even if you're one of those people who knows everything about everything (What are those people called, again? There's a great word for it.), there is so much on the president's plate that it's impossible to have the relevant facts and cogent analyses at the ready for every situation. Where is Yemen, again? Aren't there two of them? Which one is our friend? Why are we bombing them, again? These are the kinds of questions you must ask and probably not ones you can answer all by yourself.

Being a good judge of people and having cultivated a strong team of independent thinkers as advisors, I was as able, many people have said, as any president in history to deal with both ordinary day-to-day business and extraordinary events. In addition to smart, experienced go-getters, a president's core team must include confident, strong-willed individuals who will challenge decisions with contrary notions and worst-case scenarios. Thinking about what might go wrong with a particular course of action is essential. How many of the regrettable decisions made by past presidents, from ill-advised wars to unwanted space shuttle explosions, could have been avoided if only someone had said, "Now, wait a minute . . ."

That point bears a little elaboration.

As valuable as it can be to hear alternative and opposing viewpoints, I think we all know that there are certain people in this world, some of them reasonably smart or, at least, good with words, who get an unwholesome "kick" out of disagreeing with other people and constantly trying to prove them wrong or just confuse them with "but"s and "what if"s. I honestly have no use for these kinds of people. Even when the advice they're giving has some basis in fact, you just can't get the idea that they're bringing up some problem or issue just to be annoying and show how smart they are. Government is full of these kinds of aggravating smarty pants, and unfortunately, because of my deep belief in the importance of always hearing the unvarnished truth, I have sometimes ended up with one or two of them in my inner circle.

The lesson for anyone reading this who is considering a career in government is to know the facts, sure, have a questioning mind, fine, but learn to feel the room a bit, too, so that you're not always "that guy" (or "girl"!) who slows down every decision and makes every meeting run longer than it's supposed to. There's a fine line between being conscientious and being a self-centered narcissist who always makes everything all about you. If you're working for the president, it's not like anyone's going to blame you anyway. They always blame the president for anything that goes wrong. Anything. It's not fair, it sucks, and your stupid know-it-all objections really aren't helping.

In order to illustrate the sort of decision-making process that I typically followed while president, which is something my publisher thinks people might be very interested in, let me give you a hypothetical example of a crisis and walk you through how I would resolve it. So, what's a good hypothetical example of a crisis? Thinking. Okay, how about this: After years of brutal military dictatorship, the small African nation of Bugumba democratically elected the former opposition leader, Joseph Mbaba, as its president. Mbaba ruled increasingly autocratically, enriching his family and cronies at the expense of his desperately poor nation. In order to do that, he made deals with a number of international conglomerates, including some American ones, to exploit the country's mineral wealth, in particular, its large deposits of cobalt, which is used in the manufacture of electronics, especially cell phones, and also solar panels, which are essential for a clean-energy future.

When he was campaigning for office, Joseph Mbaba pledged that he would serve no more than two four-year terms, but now, as the end of his second term approaches, he is showing no signs of preparing to preside over the election of a successor. Instead, he has been making inflammatory speeches about the threat posed by the People's Revolutionary Front (PRF), which has led an insurgency of poor farmers and herders in the eastern part of the country, where Bugumba shares a border with the Republic of Zongia, which is the regional power and believed to be the patron of the PRF. All signs indicate that Mbaba will declare martial law, cancel the election, and rule by decree.

So what should a president do in this situation? The United States has no vital national interests in the region, but it does have business interests, and those people are probably going to look to protect their investment at all costs, even if it means propping up the sort of dictator who dissolves his enemies in acid as their families are forced to watch. Are those American businesses with interests in Bugumba donors? Do they have good lobbyists? These are factors that would unquestionably play a role in our cash-crazy political system. Are either of the combatants radical Islamists? Well, you know what? They d-mn well might be. That's the sort of wrinkle that is always turning up in these kinds of international situations. Mbaba has probably started catering to Muslims and begun allowing them to enforce Sharia law. That's exactly the kind of thing he would do for entirely cynical reasons (although he claims to be a follower of "all" religions, it's hard to believe a guy like that believes in anything other than whatever gods support stealing, rape, and hideous public architecture).

The PRF, on the other hand, are Christians or animists, so I guess we would naturally want to support them. Trust me, f-cking evangelicals in this country love to make a big fuss about Christians being persecuted elsewhere. I guess it makes them feel like big-shot tough guys and victims at the same time. But frankly, I've pretty much given up trying to get into the heads of those a-sholes. Generally speaking, though, the United States isn't big on supporting the violent overthrow of governments, even in a place like Africa, where the residents regard that as the normal state of affairs. The thinking is that world leaders, especially the ones on the crooked and violent end of the spectrum (on the opposite end, for example, of Sweden), might be hesitant to sign treaties and let us open military bases in their country if they thought we might change our minds all of a sudden and let them have their genitals cut off and stuffed into their empty eye sockets by a violent mob. Moreover, the State Department is being their usual bitchy, sanctimonious selves about the regional and continental balance of power, and they don't want to tip things in Zongia's favor. Does that mean the State Department is going to tell you what you *should* do? Uh-uh. No way. Foggy Bottom, as I call it, is a great place to go if you want to find some *new* problems, but I would bet doubloons to donuts that the secretary of state and his State Department have never come up with a single g-ddamned *solution* in their entire two-hundred-plus year history.

So you see how hard it is to be president? Plus, maybe there are some American hostages, probably being held by the PRF. They don't give a sh-t, so they'd probably grab a few hostages if they came across some. And the thing about these hostages is that it often seems like they were the kind of people who were basically asking for it by going somewhere they weren't supposed to in the "spirit of adventure" or to save the endangered mountain tortoise or because they are self-appointed "journalists" who work for a website you've never heard of. Still, you can't just write them off, much as you might want to. You have to express concern and have your picture taken with their fat, trailer park parents, at least one of whom, I absolutely promise you, will be wearing an American flag sweater and have eccentric facial hair in a style that hasn't been seen since the Napoleonic Wars.

By the way, while you're assessing all these variables or, for that matter, just trying to figure out the basics, like where the h-ll Bugumba is on the map or whether Kululu or Rumpenda is the capital (it's Kululu), you're trying to deal with everything else a president has to do to keep the country running and advance her (or his!) agenda, not to mention all the ceremonial h-rseshit like state dinners, meeting with Girl Scouts and sports teams, or lighting the White House menorah on Menorah Day.

That's why presidents hate crises. Because there are never any good, easy solutions, but doing nothing isn't an option (even though it would probably be the best thing to do in almost every case) because then you look weak and indecisive. As soon as you look weak, those hyenas—the general public—will jump all over you and eat you alive.

What would I do in the hypothetical Bugumba situation given above? It's difficult to say. I've done such a good job of constructing a realistic scenario for you that it's hard to figure a way out. To tell you truth, I really don't like Joseph Mbaba, and I think that making a deal with him, even if it preserves the region's delicate balance of power, will just embolden him. Even if he distances himself from the Islamists now, he'll go running right back to them the next time there's trouble. Sooner or later, the a-shole is going to start a real shooting war and cause a massive refugee crisis, which, of all the different kinds of crisis, I can assure you is the absolute *worst*.

But that example was a little hard, because the crisis was slow-moving and slowly building. So let's take another hypothetical example, this time of the more "classic" type that features a sudden, unexpected development requiring prompt action, as opposed to end-less, meandering briefings in unnecessary detail from pompous life-long civil servants unable to conceal their pleasure in themselves.

Let's try again:

The small, impoverished Central American nation of San Cris-tobel has an uneasy relationship with the United States due to some unwelcome attention from the CIA back in the 1960s. Neverthe-less, San Cristobel is almost entirely dependent on the United States because remittances from Cristobelians (as they are called) working in the States, foreign aid, and a nascent bullsh-t ecotourism industry in the country's small rain forest constitute the bulk of the national economy. The country's new president, Diego Monteverde, a hand-some former college professor (warning sign!) with leftist leanings, has been giving speeches about "breaking the shackles of colonialism" and "declaring the death of dollar diplomacy," blah blah blah, you know the kind of thing I'm talking about.

Normally, we wouldn't be paying a lot of attention to President Monteverde's commie rantings. In fact, we would be attempting to deny him the oxygen of publicity by studiously ignoring him. The last thing we'd want is some anti-American firebrand on the cover of *Time* magazine with one of their dumb cover lines like "San Cristobel: The Flaming Bag of Dog Sh-t on America's Doorstep" or something.*

Unfortunately, thanks to a ridiculous screwup by the Navy, one of our state-of-the-art spy ships, which is supposed to be invisible to radar, turned out to be a little *too* invisible and crashed into two fishing boats, sinking one of them. Two fishermen drowned, and even

---

* I swear that there is nothing sadder than *Time* magazine's feeble efforts to stay relevant and not just something that you used to read on grandma's toilet when you were disposing of Thanksgiving dinner.

though the ship, the USS *Norvell Ward*, rescued the rest of their crews, the damage was done. So far so good, right? But, yet again, as in the Bugumba example, there were complications. For starters, one of the fishermen on the other boat dragged out an old Lee-Enfield bolt-action rifle of a type that, though long out of date, is extremely reliable even when wet and fired off a few shots at what he later claimed he thought was a sea monster. The crew of the *Ward*, thinking they were under attack, opened up with their 5"/54-caliber deck gun, completely missing the guy who had shot at them (of course) but killing three others.

And then one of the seemingly inevitable complications that always seem to arise in these hypothetical scenarios arose. The commander of the *Ward*, Lieutenant Commander Evelyn Ng, the first Vietnamese American woman to command a capital ship in American history, thinking that the fishing boat captains were unlikely to have the means to contradict her, tinkered with her log book to suggest that she was actually outside of the territorial waters of San Cristobal when the accident occurred. I understand why she did it, even if it was wrong, and it should be pointed out that, by doing so, she was not just attempting to cover her own a-s but the enormous a-s of the United States of America.

For a moment, it seemed like the whole thing might blow over, with a simple payment to the families of the deceased men. But then the San Cristobal Air Force (that's something I would pay good money to see!) released a set of radar intercepts showing that the *Ward* was actually much closer to the shoreline than Lt. Cmdr. Ng had claimed and made a formal protest. The Navy issued a vague denial and, in response, the Cristobalians revealed that the ship had actually been hovering just offshore for weeks, presumably eavesdropping on everyone's private conversations and d-ck pix.

The whole thing was rapidly snowballing out of control. Other countries in the region joined the protest, demanding that the United States pledge to respect their territorial integrity, including sovereign waters. Fishermen carrying their nets engaged in camera-ready, beautifully art directed protests (anything for a day off work, right, muchachos?), and the anti-American American press had a field day. To complicate things, Vietnamese Americans, who had celebrated Evelyn Ng's promotion as a matter of pride, now began to complain that she was being used as a scapegoat in an ugly reminder of the overt prejudice of years gone by.

In short, the hypothetical San Cristobal crisis was a real mess being made worse by professional agitators stirring things up to make political hay. To compound the problem, the people of San Cristobal are proud, very proud, and even if President Monteverde was prepared to settle the whole thing with some quiet, private diplomacy, the crowds on the streets of the capital, Santa Rosa de Flores, screaming "Yankee go home" in their native tongue, whatever that was, were not about to let him.

The solution? Boy, that's tough. Maybe just promote Lt. Cmdr. Ng to full commander and transfer her to an obscure desk job somewhere, keep the payoffs to the locals coming, and wait for the whole thing to blow over. I'd consider sending an extra $100 million of foreign aid but, frankly, I don't trust that oily President Monteverde any farther than I could throw him, which, in no small part due to his oiliness, probably wouldn't be very far.

It's not a perfect plan, but it's the best I can come up with on short notice.

I hope you can see from these realistic examples how hard it is to cope with crises when you're president. Maybe you have things in your life that seem like big crises to you (you crashed your car, your dog needs an expensive operation, your kid is shooting heroin) and think they're much harder to deal with because you don't have a lot of aides and experts like the president does. Well, I can tell you from personal experience that having all these people around you doesn't make things easier. It makes things harder, because at first you believe in them, and then they let you down.

And, at least when you're dealing with your problems, you don't have the nitpickers and Monday morning quarterbacks second-guessing your every decision. During the very real crises I encountered in office, like the Leon West Tehran Hostage Rescue or the Banking Crisis of 2016, I made dozens of decisions, and I probably stand by a lot of them. But the best advice I can give you about dealing with crises, real or hypothetical, is to avoid them in the first place.

CHAPTER ELEVEN

No "I" in "Team"—
The Wind Beneath My Wings

Everyone knows that there is no "i" in "team." If they don't, I think they probably learned it when I said it somewhere earlier in this book. But there is a "me" in "team." You have to rearrange the letters a bit, but it's definitely there. I guess by the same token there is "meat" in "team," too.

The "me" in my team was me. Every president has advisors, official and unofficial, and aides, of course, and every so often one of them, like Henry Kissinger, will achieve a level of prominence and renown that approaches that of the president himself (or herself!), though I doubt whoever the president was back then liked being eclipsed by Henry Kissinger very much. In my case, I often found that my closest, most loyal advisors were useful for making suggestions that I could do the opposite of. Still, I would be remiss if I did not acknowledge them and offer up a few observations about their personalities and choice anecdotes about our time working together.

First and foremost, there is that great grumpy bear of a man Ben Cafferty and his constant companion and alter-ego, Kent Davison. There are many others. Karen Collins. Others.

On second thought, I don't think I really need to spend a lot of time on observations and anecdotes here. They can do that in their own books.

CHAPTER TWELVE

On the Run Again—
Campaigning in the "Real" America

Attentive readers will recall that although I was now, in fact, the president, I was also still running *for* president. With Election Day less than a year away, the most intense part of the campaign season had already begun when President Hughes decided to step down. As president, of course, I now had considerable advantages over the competition, most importantly the power of incumbency and the ability to generate headlines and earn free media coverage on a daily, sometimes hourly, basis. Now, anyone in the public eye knows that fame and political prominence have two sides, and the press is as ready to criticize and find petty faults as they are to be supportive. In fact, they're generally much more eager to condemn than they are to praise. But once you've met a few of the reporters who cover the White House and see what pathetic and depressing retards* they are, you'll see why they can't resist the urge to try and bring someone else down. I've

---

* I know this word is not regarded as "politically correct" when used metaphorically. However, I am using it literally here. I believe that most of these people would be clinically disgnosed by established experts as mentally retarded and I don't know anyone who has spent a lot of time around the White House press corps who feels otherwise.

always maintained that the best sort of people don't go into journalism, finding it generally too disgusting on all levels.

In fact, all media people fall into two categories: attractive morons (TV reporters usually) and unattractive morons (print, radio, the "internet"). Whenever I speak to press groups or to reporters individually, I always ask why reporters are all so stupid and just kind of weak—not, mind you, in order to be insulting, but because I'm honestly curious—and they always laugh idiotically or just stare at me uncomprehendingly. Frankly, it turns out that the press are actually just about the worst people to ask to explain why the press is so dumb and embarrassing, which is pretty ironic when you hear how much they talk about the importance of investigative reporting and being honest.

Still, some people believe that there's no such thing as bad publicity or, as George M. Cohan once said, more or less, "I don't care what they print as long as they spell my name right"—though supposedly that was because he was a virulent anti-Semite and wanted to be sure no one misspelled the Mick Irish name of Cohan as the invariably Hebraic Cohen. In the year of my presidency, I would test the theory that there is no such thing as bad publicity repeatedly and come to the conclusion that, yes, actually, there *is* such a thing as bad publicity.

And I got plenty of it.

The processes of retail politicking were different for me as president than they were for the wet-behind-the-ears Congressional candidate of a decade earlier. I had the "bully pulpit" of the presidency at my disposal, from which I could bully people, and bully them I did. I no longer had to ring doorbells and risk encountering bad smells or people wearing cheap clothes from Target or, sometimes, Goodwill. I also found that many more people, though not everyone, knew who I was and, if they didn't know who I was, I could explain that I was the president, which is much easier for people to grasp and sounds much more impressive than saying that you're someone's congressman or senator.

This is not to say that campaigning is actually fun or enjoyable as president just because it's *more* fun and *more* enjoyable than doing it as a something-other-than-president. Still, it must be endured, since voters and the media expect it. The trick is to try and keep it to a bare minimum, until the time comes when robots can take over, a day that every politician will agree cannot come soon enough.

Actually, there's another trick.

This is a good one, and one that can be used in pretty much any unpleasant situation, not just campaigning. If you learn nothing more from reading this book than this one trick (along with the "horrible/ delicious" one I mentioned earlier), it will have been worth whatever you paid for it, even if you bought the hardcover.

As one of the many horribly sexist customs that still prevails in Congress even now in the twenty-first century, if you are a female legislator you are supposed to show a more-than-usual interest in hearings having to do with sexual assault, just as male congressmen and senators are supposed to be particularly interested in hearings involving firearms or interstate trucking. And sexual assault is not one of those topics, like confirming an ambassador or deciding whether or not to land on the moon, that eventually gets resolved one way or the other. The hearings just go on and on with seemingly endless permutations having to do with where and how the sexual assault takes place: sexual assault on campus, sexual assault in prison, sexual assault in the workplace, et cetera, et cetera, et cetera, ad nauseum.

One day back when I was in the House or Senate, I can't remember exactly, I was sitting in my umpteenth hearing about sexual assault, doodling on my special congressional notepad, my mind wandering restlessly, when the woman who was testifying, I can't remember if she was a victim or some kind of expert like a doctor or professor or maybe she was both, anyway, whoever she was she said something that made my ears perk up instantly and I will never forget it.

She was explaining various methods for coping with the psychological trauma that generally accompanies sexual assaults, and she described a process she (or he? I'm pretty sure it was a she) called "positive mnemonic visualization," in which one thinks of some pleasant memory from one's past instead of whatever *unpleasant* thing is happening at the moment. I immediately put this technique to use by remembering a trail ride I had taken in Jackson Hole one summer with Daddy when we traveled through fields of wildflowers up to a peak from which we had a spectacular view of the Tetons. Daddy, as I'm sure I mentioned, was a handsome man, but he always looked especially rugged and masculine in the outdoors and never more so than when he was on horseback. For the rest of that day's sexual assault testimony, I was able to appear alert and interested even though my thoughts were far away in space and time remembering the gentle motion of Daddy's strong shoulders as he sat tall in the saddle above his horse's muscular, rolling buttocks.

Unfortunately, a single memory, no matter how rich and enticing, is not sufficient to last one through an entire campaign season, when one must deal with so many boring people and events that you'll want to deep-throat a shotgun forty times a day. Fortunately, I had a whole suite of pleasant reminiscences that I utilized during my presidential campaign to get me through countless tedious encounters.

One winter when I was still a junior associate at Maltby, Pierpont, and Blumfeld, I was laboring in the Trusts and Estates department, which attracts exactly the sort of fourth-rate legal minds you would expect, when Edgar Giddings, one of the more senior partners, asked to see me. I went to his office expecting the usual armload of paperwork and a-s-grabbery when he surprised me by asking if my passport was up to date. I said that it was, and he told me to clear my schedule for the next two weeks because we were going to Europe.

The timing was fortuitous, since Andrew and I were having one of the periodic hiccoughs in our relationship that occurred from time to time. In this particular case, Andrew was on a rare winning streak thanks to an innovative Ponzi scheme called "the Airplane Game" that had netted him almost $50,000. Instead of using the money to repay what he owed me for a series of promissory notes he had forged my signature on, he had purchased a second-hand luxury Mercedes executive van and hired a driver named Manny, both of which he described as "productivity tools." When Manny crashed the van into some kind of Mexican parade while drunk and turned out to have several outstanding warrants for his arrest and also be an illegal alien to boot, well, Andrew wound up in the doghouse. At least he had insurance.

Of course, he didn't have insurance. Still, for him, the whole thing counted as a winning streak.

So I was happy for a chance to get away for a bit while he manufactured documents or fiddled with the speedometer or bribed witnesses or changed his identity or did whatever he had to do, even if it was with Edgar, who was pretty old but still appeared to be in decent shape and maybe worth at least a hand job if he took things reasonably slowly and didn't just put a blanket over his lap and demand it right after take-off, like so many guys do.

En route to Frankfurt (in proper first class, not some business bullsh-t), Edgar explained that one of the firm's clients was a German businessman by the name of Graf von Kronintorp-Fesselheim, who rewrote his will every few months to punish or reward various worthless members of his family and, having experienced the ruthless efficiency of the Allies during World War II as a colonel in the Wehrmacht, he preferred to have American lawyers do it. Although the count (*graf* means "count") was old and enfeebled and confined to a wheelchair, he still enjoyed what Edgar, in his Princeton Class of 1952 way, referred to as a "well-turned ankle." Hence my presence. All in all, it sounded like a pretty nice little junket: two weeks of room service and very lightweight legal work and, thus far into the flight, not a hand job in sight!

The count turned out to be pretty much your garden-variety Bond villain living in luxury in a *schloss* full of hunting trophies and some pretty good paintings that were probably acquired at a steep discount in the late 1930s, if you know what I'm saying. He took an instant shine to me and, somewhat to Edgar's annoyance, dismissed him early on, saying that he preferred to work with me alone because he thought Edgar looked like an anteater (which he sort of did). Edgar was getting his hourly fee whether he rewrote codicils in the castle or jacked off to the amazing hard-core porn they show on regular television in Germany back at the hotel, so, although he was mildly insulted, he didn't really give a sh-t.

The count changed his mind about his will on a pretty much hourly basis, and every change was explained to me by means of a very lengthy anecdote or two that would begin with something like, "I was thinking that I really need to do something for Helmut, my nephew I was telling you about, who is the transvestite race car driver. He is terrible with money and spends as many years as he is old in millions of euros for his birthday party every year. Even though his ears were burned off in a crash, he will live to be one hundred and will have to spend a hundred million euros for a party he will not even be able to hear. Ach, he is so worthless, but I promised his mother I would always take care of him. She was not really my sister, but a prostitute I pretended was my sister so that she could visit me in the POW camp. She was the only woman I ever loved. I think I will leave Helmut the hydroelectric plant in Schleswig-Holstein. It is a cash cow . . ." And so on like that, hour after hour, day after day. Still, it was a lot more entertaining than being stuck in some dull office doing something utterly useless like removing staples or taking depositions.

As the end of the fortnight drew near, the count informed Edgar that he couldn't possibly be finished with his revisions in the near future and that Edgar could go home while I would stay to complete the work. To speed the process, I would move into the castle. Edgar ran up his expense account for a few more days and then duty-freed his way home, leaving me and the count and two dozen servants pretty much alone in the enormous palace. Heinrich, as he insisted I call him, liked to work on the will for a few hours around midday and then send me into town to shop for a new dress or get my hair done at one of the many establishments where he had an unlimited line of credit. I would join him for dinner, for which he always wore one of his old-fashioned wing-collared tuxedo shirts and either a dinner jacket or sometimes a smoking jacket made of dark purple velvet.*

When I sat down at the dinner table, I would usually find a small box with some exquisite jewel at my place, except on Thursdays when he always gave me perfume. I recall sitting there one night wearing a shimmering gray Balenciaga gown I had bought that afternoon and a delicate pair of diamond and emerald earrings with a matching

---

* I will share a little secret with you: Until I met Heinrich, I had always hated wing-collared dress shirts, finding them just a little too "look at me, I'm in the Gay Men's Chorus!" but on him they seemed authentic and refined.

necklace, eating a roast quail stuffed with figs, as Ludwig the butler poured me a third glass of an ancient Cheval Blanc while a small orchestra played Schubert's highly evocative *Arpeggione Sonata* behind a screen and thinking, "You know, maybe being a lawyer isn't so bad after all." But of course, this couldn't last forever, and it didn't.

It got better.

The change came suddenly one night as we were playing cribbage (a particular favorite of the count's) in one of the grand salons after dinner and drinking a honeyed Sauternes in front of a roaring fire. Ludwig entered and solemnly announced that his serene highness, the Prince de Longueville, had arrived and would like to see the count. The count laughed and said something and then translated for me. "I told him to send the little c-cksucker in but to make sure he was properly dressed first," he said, then added, "They'll all be coming out of the woodwork now." He explained that the prince was another relative, one of his innumerable sons or step-daughters or great-nephews or fourth cousins who were the product of his eleven marriages. "They've heard I'm rewriting the will again, and they want to try and protect their piece of the strudel!"

A few moments later, a good-looking thirtyish Frenchman with a long nose entered in black tie and bowed to the count and kissed my hand. He did not seem even remotely surprised to find me there and offered up some brief token explanation about having been in the neighborhood and wanting to pay his respects to his dear step-great-grandfather-in-law. The count, looking amused, insisted that the prince must stay for a few days and do a bit of shooting because, since he had been confined to the wheelchair, he had been unable to tackle the pheasants himself and they were now running amok. Plus, he added mischievously, he thought I might be getting bored and might like a companion to show me around the estate.

The prince seemed to like this plan just fine, having assumed that the count had fallen under my sway and that I held the keys to his financial future. And so we passed a very happy week wandering around the countryside on foot or on horseback shooting birds and talking of our lives in a way that became surprisingly intimate very quickly. I still wonder whether I could have been truly happy with Claude de Longueville. He was an elegant and cultured man, a true deep thinker, and a sensitive and caring lover, but he was also prone to melancholy and had that somewhat resigned air of the fin-de-siècle about him. I think the fact that we both knew it would not last was perhaps what made us so open and so tender toward one another. And although he could not have anticipated what would happen next, what would turn out to be our final night together was imbued with a wistful sense of farewell. For this, too, could not last forever, and it, also, did not.

It got better.

The very next morning, as the count and I were reviewing the latest changes in his will, a hideous racket arose from the front of the house. "It is Enrico," sighed the old man. "I knew it was just a matter of time." Enrico, it turned out, was the Marchese Albergonza, another relative—an Italian who arrived in an extremely noisy yellow Ferrari that, he declared, was the only thing besides mozzarella cheese that Italians made that was worth a "Fiddler's f-ck." Instead of a demure kiss on the hand, he grabbed me by the side of my face and kissed me full on the lips, saying that having cheated death three times on the roads on the way here, he desperately needed a woman. He and Claude clearly loathed each other but kept a chilly, formal peace in the count's presence.

That night at dinner Enrico squeezed my knee and then my thigh and then ran his hand over and eventually under my panties as I attempted to make conversation and keep a straight face. Later, as I went up the stairs to my bedroom, where I expected to find Claude waiting, Enrico caught me on the landing and kissed me, hard. "You are the most enticing woman I have ever met!" he whispered urgently. "Come away with me! Come away with me now!"

And so I did.

It was madness, of course. I had no clothes other than the evening gown I was wearing and nothing else, not even a toothbrush. But he told me not to worry, that his step-uncle would send everything or, if he didn't, he, Enrico, would buy me new and "even more beautiful" things. I knew, of course, that his main reason for abducting me was not my irresistible allure but rather a desire to get me away from the count and Claude before I could make any more changes in the will. And you know what? I didn't care! Where Claude had been sad and a bit grim, Enrico was carefree and full of life.

When we roared down the long poplar-lined drive leading from the Schloss Kronintorp-Fesselheim, I don't think Enrico had any real plan for where he was going to take me. But since the road pointed in that direction anyway, he declared that we must go skiing while the snow was still good before spring set in in earnest. Over the next few weeks, we skied at St. Moritz, Gstaad, and, my personal favorite, the small, exclusive resort of Cortina d'Ampezzo in the Dolomites. Everywhere we went, Enrico was known, was beloved, and was a cause for wild, decadent, all-night parties with a glamorous, jet-set crowd of dukes and princes and barons and their equally glamorous duchesses, princesses, and baronesses.*

---

* I should point out that, having endured a brief and expensive first marriage to a phony Italian prince herself, the one useful piece of information my mother drilled into me from an early age was that all European titles except English

In short, the whole thing was an empty fraud, but it was also a chic, charming, and quintessentially European fraud, and I, for one, could see no percentage in blowing the whistle on anyone. Why would I? I was having the time of my life. First of all, skiing in Europe, where most of the resorts are built near glaciers and where most of the trails are above the tree line, is infinitely better than skiing in America. I don't care where you've been—Aspen, Stowe, Sun Valley— they all eat a-s in prison compared with even a second-rate place like Zermatt. And after the skiing ended, the next season—boar-hunting season—began. Enrico and I would see some of the same people but also always delightful new people as we shot boars from the Black Forest all the way down to Tuscany. As those of you who read the earlier parts of this book and didn't just skip lazily to this part will know, I've always loved all kinds of hunting, but I think boar hunting will always be my favorite. Something about seeing something move

ones (and you had to be a little careful about those, too) were fake and that these people were no more legitimate aristocrats than Porky, Duke of Pig. When Italy, France, and Germany lost their crowned heads, they also lost their legitimate founts of honor, leaving every Tomassino, Ricard, and Harald free to call themselves whatever they wanted to. If they were rich enough, they could usually get another person to go along with the charade, and two or three generations later the whole thing seemed as real as King Arthur. Or maybe more real than that. When the gruff but lovable Kaiser departed for exile, he took with him any notion of restraint on the part of the aspiring merchant classes, who quickly ennobled themselves with varying degrees of ballsiness. The count's ancestors, who had built an enormous chemicals empire, thought they ought to be *grafs* and, presto, so they were. The situation was much the same in France, where three different ruling families and the Napoleonic Code by doing away with primo geniture and entail had encouraged every farmer to become a baron or better. And the situation in Italy was the usual sh-t show one can expect from the Italians. All this and more, my mother explained to me over and over, night after night, determined that I would not make the same mistake she had as a young woman, very nearly ruining her life by trusting in the validity of a European's noble title.

in the distance, hearing the dogs bark, and then suddenly the fiesty little boar rushes out of the undergrowth and *pow!* Another one bites the dust.

Once we had exhausted the supply of boars, Enrico and I moved on to Capri, where summer was just beginning. We spent lazy, sunny days swimming, water skiing, and making love in his lovely little villa overlooking the sea. And it was there, one afternoon, when we received word that Graf von Kronintorp-Fesselheim had died and left all his money to a local cat hospital. I packed my bags quickly and caught the next flight back to Washington. Enrico had the good manners to wave goodbye to me from the bed as he talked animatedly into the phone and, for that, I will always love him.

So, there you have it. Those are the "go-to" memories I rely on when I have to try and endure one of the many unbearable aspects of being a politician. I can tell you, I got d-mn good use out of them on the campaign trail that year, and I don't think any one of those people I met at churches or union halls or town meetings ever imagined that the whole time I was standing there with the warm and happy expression on my face it was because I was actually thousands of miles away schussing down the Col Druscié in Cortina.

CHAPTER THIRTEEN

Making Even More History—
The Tie Heard 'Round the World

Like the "Holy Roman Empire," the Electoral College is neither a "college" nor "electoral." Like everyone else, I learned about it in school, and like everyone else, I never really understood what it was; in fact I eventually began to understand it a negative amount, though it was explained to me repeatedly. There's a simple reason why no one understands how the Electoral College works, and it's not because they're stupid or lazy. It's because it was devised more than two hundred years ago by men who wore powdered wigs and enormous colorful codpieces and who loved to argue about airy-fairy ideas that would be a giant annoying nuisance for centuries to come while picking lice off of one another and eating them like those monkeys in the zoo with the swollen red a-ses. Mr. Eggerston, my eleventh grade history teacher, one of the few truly honest teachers I ever had, taught me the real, unvarnished truth about the Founding Fathers and what pigs they were, and I've never forgotten it. "Eggs" was a garden-variety prep school drunk and pervert who undoubtedly drilled more than his share of locker room peepholes, but he had a real gift for teaching.

Wherever they are burning in hell, I bet the founding fathers still enjoy an occasional laugh, in between the screams, when they think about the Electoral College.

Election Night is supposed to be the end of a presidential campaign. In 2016, though, it was just the beginning, or rather just the middle, or maybe just the beginning of the end.

The race had been extremely close all along. While I make no excuses, I was handicapped in making a mark as president by the short duration of my presidency, by opposition from glory-hound legislators and the corrupt media, as well as the incompetence of some of my staff. My opponents, their surrogates, and other haters seized upon the "accidental president" line of attack, as though I had won some sort of presidential reality show and not previously served as vice president, senator, and congresswoman. Had I been a man, I'm sure they would not have acted like my presidency was a mere fluke and best forgotten quickly.

Although I am often critical of the voters, the polls showed that some of them, at least, were not as dumb as they appeared to be. Enough of them seemed to "get me" to create a "Selina Meyer base." We did some research into this group to find out what their core concerns were. Some of the comments that came back frequently were a desire to "shake sh-t up" and "f-ck yeah" and also avoid burdening the taxpayer the moving costs associated with changing presidents. That gave us something to build on.

My opponent was Arizona senator William O'Brien, who had been an irritating thorn in my side ever since I had risen to national prominence. I think even Bill O'Brien's best friends would describe him as an amiable dunce. He was very much a throwback to the bad old days of the smoke-filled room and coke-filled hooker. Still, despite that, he wasn't even remotely charming. Fat and bushy, he looked like an overstuffed antique armchair suitable for display in one of those rooms in the Smithsonian that no one goes into that are full of thing like colonial spinning wheels or lighthouse bulbs. He smelled a bit like an overstuffed armchair, as well, in particular like one that he himself had been sitting in.

Senator O'Brien's running mate was New Mexican spitfire Laura Montez, who had been recruited to add a little "color" to the ticket, since O'Brien came off as white as Uncle Ben's rice after it had been converted a few dozen times. Race and ethnicity are rightly considered an electrified "third rail" sitting on a bed of live wires in American politics and can rarely be addressed directly without causing an enormous amount of pearl clutching and panty twisting. That's why I couldn't come right out and say that she had been born and raised in Connecticut and was no more Mexican than Bill O'Brien was. Or, to put it another way, she was a true "new" Mexican, having become a Mexican right before entering politics.

The former Laura Cunningham had made a shrewd and cynical political calculation and entered into a presumably loveless marriage of convenience with Alejandro Montez, a good-looking and very gay-seeming slip-and-fall shyster and minor-league politician in his own right. Somehow they'd managed to conceive a few attractive children, and I have to admit that they made a wholesome counterpoint to the boozy and bloated O'Brien, who always seemed to have a little bit of dried vomit on his King Tut beard.

On my side, I had my associate of long standing, the famously craggy and charming Tom James.

Tom James. What to say about Tom James?

First of all, I want to make it crystal clear that I like Tom personally. Always have, always will. I also think he's intelligent and has an understanding of politics that is both instinctual and the product of years of experience. He's hard-working and connects easily with all sorts of people, not just those from a similar tweedy Northeastern background. He's also quite good looking and has a sort of lanky, shambling gait that makes him irresistible to women. These are just some of the reasons why I chose him over my serving vice president, Andrew Doyle, who seemed worn out and has probably seemed worn out since his mom finished labor. Andrew served his country well, or at least okay, but if you just Google a picture of Andrew and compare it to a picture of Tom, you'll see that it was really no contest. The picture will also remind you to get your prostate checked because, true to the stereotype of the prostate, that bothersome walnut-sized gland that sits proudly between a man's anus and his testicles proved to be a problem for Andrew, as it is for so many men who look like Andrew.

Those are the reasons I chose Tom. So, what are the reasons that I shouldn't have chosen him? Well, for one thing, he's a vicious, unscrupulous snake in the grass with a sick pathological need to betray those who show him kindness. Do you remember Ted Bundy? He was the craggy and charming serial killer who lured his victims by preying on their sympathies. He would walk around college campuses with his arm in a sling or cast and ask coeds to help him carry some books or put a sailboat into a Volkswagen (who would fall for that??) before cutting their heads off and moving in with their decomposing bodies. Anyone who is considering a career in politics *really* should read up extensively on Ted Bundy to get a handle on the sort of people, like Tom James, who you'll encounter, but just to reiterate, I like Tom personally.

Election Night turned into Election Night*mare*, and then Election Morning and then Election Week and, eventually, Election Month—all thanks to the flawless system devised by the incredibly overrated founding fathers that is the envy of countries across the globe . . . not! After conceding and then unconceding on Election Night, things initially looked pretty promising. I had won the popular vote, which, though it doesn't count for as much as it should, still gives you the high ground as far as public opinion, since the other guy has to explain all the Electoral College nonsense, which always makes it sound like you're trying to win on a sneaky technicality.

At first it seemed like we might be able to resolve the whole matter quickly and in my favor due to some irregularities in, no surprise, Nevada, the perennial runner-up to Florida in the Miss Crazy State Pageant. The post office, which seems to take mail-in ballots for president less seriously than they do "20% Off" coupons from Bed Bath & Beyond, had misplaced thousands of ballots. But when they were eventually discovered in the trunk of a pre-rampage former postal worker, they were not in my favor and simply perpetuated the stalemate (and also lost me the popular vote) while forcing me to now clutch at the very thin reed of the aforementioned Electoral College.

For a normal, rational person like me, counting on the Electoral College was like having to rely on some other inexplicable force, like gravity. Once you start thinking about it all the time, it becomes extremely nerve-racking. Not only that, although it wasn't clear whether I was the president-elect, it was completely clear that I was still the president, and I was determined to continue to do that job as well as I could while there was still a chance I might remain in office. That meant coping with a financial crisis brought on by uncertainty over the outcome of the election, dealing with a deadly salmonella outbreak caused by Thanksgiving turkeys, and nonstop cyberattacks from the Chinese, who peppered my gullible staff mercilessly with notices of Irish sweepstakes winnings. Before long, the White House servers had more viruses and less privacy than one of those bathhouses where men go to catch viruses in public.

It was a turbulent time in my private life, as well. Presidents have, well, certain *needs*, needs that are perhaps greater than those of ordinary people. One of the stories I used to enjoy telling visitors to the Oval Office was that the appetites of Louis XIV, France's famous "Sun King," were so enormous that when he died the doctors doing his autopsy discovered that his large intestine was twice as large as a normal large intestine. It was not simply a "large" intestine; it was a *huge* intestine.

Though I have no reason to believe that my large intestine is any larger than normal, I share the tendency toward outsized appetites that distinguishes great leaders: Churchill's love for cigars, for example, or Catherine the Great's fondness for f-cking horses. During a (low-calorie) lunch with historians at the White House,* I was asked if a female president needed to be loved more than a male president. At the time I couldn't think of a good answer. And then, after the historians left, I actually thought of a good answer. Not just a good answer, a *great* answer, and I thought immediately, "Sh-t! I should write that down so I don't forget it." But then something happened or someone came in and, sure enough, I forgot my great answer.

The thing is that although the sexes are equal, women are much needier than men. We just are. And we might as well embrace it. No one likes a needy man. No one likes a needy woman, either, but they

---

* This was something we tried once, assuming it would be catnip for the press— and it was—but never did again after one of the historians ended up talking too much.

dislike her less than they dislike a needy man. The thing most people don't realize is that neediness is actually a form of strength. In many respects, it is the greatest form of strength, because when you are needy, you make it clear what you *need* from others. And setting clear expectations for others is one of the most effective ways to assert power over them.

With so much pressure and drama surrounding the election, it's no wonder that I was feeling my special female neediness power extremely acutely at this time. My relationship with Charlie Baird, the white-haired wizard of Wall Street, which began in the fall of 2016, was a sophisticated executive decision on my part to address some of my needs in an efficient and professional manner. Charlie was smart, rich, and universally respected. He was also charming and funny and had his own airplane with a stand-up toilet. All in all, he was a suitable consort for a president. The sex was good, not great, due mainly, I think, to a lack of imagination on his part, which always surprised me considering how ingenious he was at inventing exotic derivative securities.*

People always ask, "What's it like to have sex in the White House? It must be really hot, right?" The answer is, "No. It's not particularly hot. Do you think it's hot to have sex in your grandmother's house? What's wrong with you?"

Eventually, the relationship had to be sacrificed on an altar of political expediency, and we parted with no more than an ordinary degree of bitterness and recrimination. There was a lot of that kind of

---

* I'm sorry if this is "too much information" or "TMZ" as it's called. The manuscript of the book that I submitted to my publisher was short of the contractually mandated amount by about twenty-six words, and I had no choice but to add an assessment of my sex life with Charlie Baird to make up the difference. I was under incredible deadline pressure and it's the only thing I could think of.

thing going on at the time, and worse: deviousness, scheming, plots within plots, the White House resembling nothing so much as the Vatican under the Borgia popes,* although I'll always have a bit of a soft spot for Callixtus III for vindicating Joan of Arc, albeit posthumously).

To the public, it must have appeared very confusing and yet not terribly interesting—sort of like a foreign film. But for us on the inside, well, we were fighting for our political lives, or at least I was. My trusted advisors seemed spectacularly unable to find a clear path to the victory that always seemed almost within my grasp. Others around me repeatedly let me down, either through sheer incompetence or a stunning degree of myopic self-centeredness that, considering the stakes, bordered on the unpatriotic—even treasonous. Chief among this latter group was my own daughter (speaking of the Borgias!). Catherine seemed to think that just when her mother was working as hard as she could to be president was an ideal time to tell me that she had decided that she was a lesbian and was dating one of my Secret Service agents.

Those of you who have children know how they always seem to ruin things by demanding time and attention with no consideration for others. I think every parent will agree that children are "takers" not "givers." Here was Catherine, twenty-three or twenty-six years of age, still sucking the life out of me just as she did during those nine endless months in the womb. Whenever she wastes my time with some petty concern of her own (and it's still happening!), I think how grateful I am that she is an only child—though I suppose things might have been different if I'd had a boy, since they seem much more self-reliant.

Am I right, moms?

---

* Who were as nasty a pair of pontiffs as you'll ever meet.

Ultimately, of course, as everyone knows, the election was stolen from me at the last minute through the sort of dishonest parliamentary maneuverings that we can also thank the founding f-ckheads for gifting us with.

The Meyer presidency was over.

EPILOGUE

A Woman in Full: Full Woman

Or was it?

Yes, it was.

The measures of a successful presidency are straightforward: a strong economy, a country and a world at peace, and enlightened initiatives to secure a better and brighter future for all Americans. The measures of a successful *post*-presidency are less clearly defined. A PPOTUS is supposed to retire gracefully from the stage and spend the rest of his (or her!) days in relative seclusion doing good works and turning up in the newspapers only when another PPOTUS dies or when he (or she!) gets into a fight with a fast-food employee or flight attendant that someone records on their cell phone.

Not me.

I have a phrase I use—it's kind of silly but I made it up years ago, and I still say it to myself softly, under my breath, when the chips are down—"Nobody puts Baby in the corner!" What I mean by that phrase is that I am "Baby" and nobody can push me aside and put me in some kind of corner. I used to use an earlier version of the phrase, which was "Nobody puts the baby in the corner!" but it evolved over time and eventually the article disappeared and "baby" became capitalized. Anyway, I don't want to lose track of what I'm trying to say, which is that nobody puts Baby in the corner, not before Baby was president, not when Baby was president, and not now when Baby has had the presidency stolen from her.

A very small number of activities are deemed appropriate for a PPOTUS. Unlike a former sports star, a PPOTUS cannot open a chain of affordable family-friendly steakhouses called "Meyer's Flaming Pit," star on Broadway in *D-mn Yankees* or even *A Night with Selina Meyer*, or become a Las Vegas casino greeter, despite the fact that Gerald Ford did it for many years. A visiting professorship at a great university, some similar post at a think tank or nongovernmental institution, the leadership of an international body such as the World Bank or UN, delivering speeches around the world, appearing in a prerecorded message at the Oscars introducing a nominated song with an anti-bullying message . . . these are the sort of things that a PPOTUS is expected to do.

And, of course, there is the obligatory book, which you are reading now.

There is also one's presidential library, and I expect that by the time you are reading this, mine has been built. In order to accomplish that, I hope that you read this book quite slowly or pick it up now and then and don't read this part until several years after it is published. I want a really *good* presidential library—one where people can get really up to their elbows in the Meyer presidency—not one that feels slapdash, cheap, superficial, or impulsive like so many others. Scholars are fortunate that I myself expect to be around for many years to assist them firsthand with their research into the Meyer Era. They will have to make an appointment, though, because I don't plan to just hang around my library waiting to be recognized. That would be pathetic. If I do do anything like that, it would be in disguise.

Thanks to some pioneering work by my recent predecessors, it is no longer necessary for a president to participate in the good works of others. He (or she!) can do her (or his!) *own* good works through a process that begins with the identification of a problem, continues with the good works themselves, and ends with the problem being solved. I think that some of the efforts of past presidents to solve world problems (I won't name names, but I'm sure you can figure out who I'm talking about) have been tainted by their committing to merely a disengaged figurehead role, by delegating excessively, or by attaching themselves, leech-like, to some existing charity like UNICEF and that kind of thing rather than taking the time and making the effort to really do something personal and original.

Hence the Meyer Fund, my new global initiative that will tackle some of the world's most intractable problems. People may love me or hate me, but I think everyone will agree that when it comes to overcoming the biggest challenges we face in the world today, there is no one better suited to lead the effort with imagination, insight, hard work, and untiring devotion to improving the lives of others. For my whole life, underlying everything I have done, is one overarching principle: love for my fellow man. I am not a religious person, per se. I consider myself more "spiritual," in the sense that I believe that there might be a Higher Power in the universe that holds certain opinions about how we should conduct ourselves down here on Earth and judges us constantly for our adherence to the ideal. And I have always believed that this Higher Power, call him (or her!) what you like—Jesus, Buddha, Muhammed, Islam, Moses, etc.—wants us to treat each other with care and respect regardless of our station in life.

It's one thing to talk about these fine, noble sentiments. It is very much another thing to attempt to live by them. I believe that, through the Meyer Fund, I will be "walking my talk" as no PPOTUS, living or dead, has ever done before. The Fund is fortunate that, at its head, it will have someone with a deep understanding of the world's problems and a strong sense of priority in terms of how to address them. First up: adult literacy.

There is an epidemic of adult illiteracy out there that simply doesn't get written about because the illiterates lack the necessary skills to describe their own misfortune. The Meyer Fund will reach out to those who suffer from this dreadful condition and hear from them in their own words or, if not words, gestures and expressive noises, what they need and want in order to become literate. That's what will set the Meyer Fund apart: It is need-based. We don't plan to patronize those we help by explaining to them what they need. We want to hear from them and then act upon the data we gather. Simple but highly innovative.

Another global problem we will be addressing is AIDS, the dreadful disease that has taken so many lives. The Meyer Fund will be leading the fight against AIDS and the search for a cure. With luck, AIDS will be cured within our lifetime, if not sooner.

Undoubtedly there will be other causes upon which the Meyer Fund turns its powerful spotlight of attention. Mine is a restless, questing intelligence unwilling to shrug my shoulders in the face of any problem. When I see something wrong, I want to fix it. I simply cannot respect people who "pass the buck" and leave messes like homelessness or Ebola (not that the Meyer Fund is working on those right now—we can't do everything!) for others to clean up. While I often find those kinds of people charming, and enjoy their devil-may-care attitude more than the scolding, sanctimonious posture of the type who will not "pass the buck," I don't really respect them.

I have never been a pessimist. Maintaining a positive attitude has gotten me through so many dark and difficult times. I truly believe that, like America, my best days are ahead of me. Fitzgerald famously said that "Every life has many acts." While, of course, I think most people agree that everyone who lives a full life does many acts in the sense of "actions," I prefer to interpret "acts" as referring to the acts of a play. If my life were a play, by my count I would currently be at the end of act 8 and looking toward the start of act 9. How many acts will there be in the drama of Selina Meyer? Only time will tell.

For now, I want the world to know both that it will not have Selina Meyer to kick around anymore and also that it has not seen the last of Selina Meyer.

Selina Meyer
Manhattan, fall, 2018

APPENDIX I

Legal Notice

Editor's note: As the consequence of a legal settlement with Catherine Meyer, Abrams Press is obligated to include the following statement in the Second Edition of A Woman First: First Woman *by Selina Meyer.*

This book is a crime against history and a crime against humanity.

My mother, Selina Meyer, has always been dishonest to a truly pathological extent. She is one of those people who can rewrite an account of an event in her mind moments after it happens that is totally at odds with what actually occurred, and then pass a lie detector test on her own version. These revisions of history are invariably made in order to flatter herself, to put herself at center stage, shift blame to others, or erase some embarrassment.

To correct the record as regards myself: I am not a selfish, spoiled brat who committed treason by telling her mother she was a lesbian at an inopportune moment, which is how I am described in this book. That is just the pot calling the kettle black—although my mother is not a lesbian. But I am not the only person defamed here. In virtually every case, my mother's descriptions of people and both her descriptions and perceptions of events are completely at odds with either what I observed directly or heard from others. In many cases, she describes events out of order or with key elements missing; in a few she invents something that didn't happen out of whole cloth.

I do not believe that this is the result of a deliberate, well-thought-out plan. My mother simply did not devote enough time and attention to this book for that to be true. After aggressively shopping a memoir for weeks, she was forced to accept a modest advance from a second-tier publisher. She then procrastinated for months and finally managed to deliver a manuscript, which she had dictated to her long-suffering press aide, Mike McLintock, over a weekend while she was under the influence of prescription drugs, nonprescription drugs, or alcohol, or some combination of all three and had recently returned from a stay in a mental hospital (or "spa," as she would have it). The result you have before you.

It has taken me many years of therapy to begin to be able to process the countless traumas my mother inflicted upon me during my childhood. My therapist believes that by airing her needling criticisms of me in public, this book may have set me back a decade in terms of dealing with my mother's damage and becoming a semi-functioning adult. The unexpected love of a good woman has been the biggest help in my healing process, and I am infinitely upset to see Marjorie Palmiotti pulled into the black hole of my mother's hatred. By buying and possibly reading this pack of lies, you are complicit in what is, quite simply, a case of child abuse.

Shame on you.

APPENDIX II

Tibet

The one thing I thought I made clear to everyone involved with this book was how important it was to be accurate and comprehensive—to "get it right the first time," as it were. This is not some book about how to organize your sweater drawer, though I hope to Chr-st it sells like one. This is a history.

But somehow things fell through the cracks, and crucial details were omitted despite my clear instructions. And not just "details." In fact, there is no mention anywhere in the book of what most people, including myself, regard as the most important achievement of my presidency, the freeing of Tibet.

Yes, Tibet. Mysterious snow-capped land of monasteries; of intriguing Lhasa; of the city that time forgot, where daily life is still conducted according to the ancient rhythms of past millennia; of dignified lamas who live in both the world of the here and now and the world of the eternal spirit; of the yak, that great domesticated bovid with the beatnik hairdo; of mountains that literally scrape the sky, true pillars of heaven including the highest and noblest of all, Everest. It is a land of great joyous festivals and silent solemn prayers—a place, it is said, where the Buddha still walks among men as long as they are willing to walk with him.

Tibet—peaceful, happy, minding-its-own-business Tibet—is also a land enslaved or, at least, it was until I freed it. Tibet's enormous neighbor, the insatiable, relentless, ruthless China, had had its billions of eyes on Tibet for hundreds of years and, once the Communist government consolidated its power in the mid-twentieth century, it began to chip away at Tibet's independence.

By the time I decided to do something about Tibet, the saintly and beloved Dalai Lama was firmly under China's thumb, and the Tibetans themselves, once so joyous and carefree, were now very sad indeed and wandered around in a listless funk. Or so I am told.*

When I imposed strict sanctions on China in 2016 in response to their hacking of the White House servers and posting of fake messages on my Twitter account that were intended to embarrass me personally, I intended for them to sting. And sting they clearly did. Lu Chi-Jang immediately began a series of overtures through intermediaries that culminated in an agreement that Tibet would be freed and the Tibetan people given the right of self-determination. Appropriately, the agreement was brokered at Camp David, where several decades before, the Camp David Accords, which reorganized the violence in the Middle East in a whole new way, were signed. Hopefully, these new Camp David Accords will work out a little better than the last ones.

Because of the extreme delicacy of the negotiations, it was not possible to announce the liberation of Tibet right away, and due to some very inopportune timing, the news was announced right as Laura Montez was being inaugurated, blurring the issue of who deserved the

---

* Despite what I just said about China, I have the utmost respect for its seemingly permanent president, Lu Chi-Jang. Though congenitally devious, like most Asians, he is not as bad as some. One can make a deal with Lu, and once the deal is made, he's probably just as likely to stick to it as you are. It all depends on a million unpredictable factors, but there's at least a chance he will at any rate.

credit. President Montez did nothing to clarify the matter and, frankly, why would she? It's not like she had anything else to brag about. It was not until the *Washington Post* ran a series of articles following the publication of the first edition of this book that my role was fully revealed and I finally got the credit I deserved for the greatest foreign policy triumph of the twenty-first century.

You'd think something like that would be a good thing to talk about in my book, right? You'd think that a book that was supposed to be about my presidency (even though it was actually mostly about my life before my presidency, because I ran out of time to write about the presidency thanks to the publisher's endless brow-beating) would at a bare minimum include the most important thing I accomplished during said presidency?? But no. It's not in there! Not a single mention! Zilch! Zippo!!

It wasn't until word got back to me from several people who read the book that Tibet was missing that I learned of the error. Now, I suppose, I have to go back and read through the whole thing to find out what other mistakes are in there. I'm glad to have a chance to add the Liberation of Tibet to this, the second edition, but sorry that I'm not able to write in more detail, because, in an entirely justified act of righteous indignation, I fired the person responsible for the error, Mike McLintock, and wasn't able to get him back here to fix his mess before the deadline for the second edition. I think we should be able to include a more comprehensive account in the third edition or, if not then, the fourth edition definitely. We will also be able to add any other missing information I discover when I go back and read the book when I have time.

In any event, I want to assure you that the person responsible has been punished, and if you're thinking you can get your money back because the first edition wasn't entirely perfect, my publisher is pretty sure you can't.

ACKNOWLEDGMENTS

So many people helped with this book that it would be impossible to mention all of them. I feel like they should be mentioned, though, since upon rereading a few portions of it prior to publication, I have come to the conclusion that the book would probably have been a lot better without their help, and I think readers should know who is to blame. But, like I say, the list is long and it's mostly people you've never heard of, and my publisher seems to think that it would be a lot to ask of potential purchasers to pay for a long list of names of people who give bad advice or have confusing, contradictory opinions. Personally, I would pay good money for a list like that because, if I'd had one, maybe I would never have hired these people in the first place. But this is one of many subjects upon which my editor, Greg Morehouse, and I disagree, and I get tired of arguing with him because he's one of those people who becomes more cheerful the more he disagrees with you, and I have always found those kinds of people very hard to get a handle on.

I do feel I should thank Greg, though, for begging me to do the book in the first place and for his continued guidance along the way. As I say, we didn't always agree, and I will believe to my dying day that the book I wanted to do, which would have been a detailed account of my early years, would have been much more interesting and, frankly, better, but he insisted that the book should be about my career in politics and, especially, as president. The result, for what it's worth, you are holding in your hands. If you agree with me, though, that the other book, the one about my childhood that I didn't get to write, would have been a lot better and more interesting, will you do me a favor and say so in a one-star review on Amazon? I'm told that that's all these publishing people care about.

My longtime colleague Mike McLintock, familiar to many of you from his White House briefings when he was my press secretary, certainly deserves a mention for the assistance he gave me in reconstructing the events of my life and in recording my thoughts about those events. Funny story about Mike: It's impossible for me to think of Mike without remembering the disgusting way he eats shrimp. In particular, I'm thinking of those kind of shrimp that have the tail still attached. Mike doesn't just bite off the shrimp above the tail like a normal person, he kind of squeezes the tail to get all the shrimp meat and juices out and then chews up the tail shell in order to make sure that there's nothing left. Shrimp tails are revolting under the best of circumstances, but a plate full of the ones that Mike has processed is something that you will never be able to forget. Picturing them now, they evoke nothing so much as the gray toenail clippings of old women who have let their toenails grow to the length of shrimp tails.

Here's why having shrimp as your "problem food" is especially bad if you work for a politician: You get it everywhere. A plate full of shrimp with a bowl of cocktail sauce in the center is exactly the kind of "fake fancy" dish that's served at banquets, fundraisers, and in green rooms across the country, including many places that are thousands of miles from the nearest live shrimp habitat. And Mike loves shrimp even more than he loves other kinds of free food. Whenever he would see a plate of shrimp, he would say, "Hey, shrimp!" or "All right, shrimp!" or "Oh, great, shrimp! I'm starving." Hearing Mike say the word "shrimp" invariably makes my stomach heave, and then having to watch him as he stations himself next to the plate of shrimp and chain smokes them is something one simply can't unsee.

I don't particularly like or dislike shrimp, or at least, I *didn't* until I saw Mike eat a few, but in those few seconds he ruined shrimp and, to some extent, all shellfish for me forever. So, thanks, Mike! Thanks a lot for that.

Finally, I definitely want to thank the one person who has never let me down, Richard Splett. Richard is the sort of whip-smart political "natural" who has a deep understanding of both people and politics. But never let that amiable exterior fool you. Inside, the man is a killer! Although Richard did not work directly on the book, I feel like the better parts of it were inspired by the transformative influence he has on pretty much everything just by virtue of his proximity.

Thank you, Richard. God bless you.

INDEX